TRANSLATED BY RISHI SINGH GHERWAL

Yoga Vasistha

Contents

One

SRI RAM, THE TRUTH SEEKER

Ram, who had acquired a great deal of knowledge, asked his father, the King, if he might make a pilgrimage to the Holy Land known as the Sacred Ashrams. His father granted him this wish. When he returned some time later, there was a decided change in his mood. It had been his custom to rise early in the morning and follow the daily ceremonies of his religion, but now instead of practicing his usual habits of worship, he sat in the Padmasana posture and assumed an indifferent attitude to all things.

Raja Rishi Viswamitra arrived at the King's palace. The King saluted the Raja Rishi and paid him great respect. He then bestowed greater marks of honor upon him, by saying: "By your visit all my sins, misery and unhappiness have been removed. Tell me, what is your need?"

Therefore, Raja Rishi said: "O King of Kings, true to your Master, Rishi Vashisht, an embodiment of justice, I came seeking the services of your son, Ram. I cannot bear the injustice forced upon me by the Rakshasan, for they do not permit me to do any good work."

The King answered him thus: "My son is indeed very young and is not trained in the area of fighting. He does not seem to be himself at this time and has become indifferent to the world. Life would become bitter and unhappy, to me and my family, should anything happen to my son, Ram. Therefore, in his stead, I will go with you, and with my army I shall meet the Rakshasan in battle."

Raja Rishi Viswamitra with great anger said: "Tell me truthfully and without faltering, if you, the King, will perform such beastly acts of deception, who will keep his word? I shall go back from where I came to endure the injustice of the Rakshasan. You may live happily with your son and others."

The great sage Rishi Vashisht said: "O King of Kings, keep your word, for your sacred duty is to protect your subjects, and let there be no injustice at any price. Your son will be safe with the Rishi Viswamitra. Your son is impassive and unconcerned toward worldly things, and his association with this Great Raja Rishi will be a great enlightenment to him. Send him forth and do not reveal the knowledge of his departure to his brothers. His indifferent state of mind, toward the world and life, is not the result of disappointment in his desires, but is a longing for liberation, which is a stepping-stone toward self-realization. When all the delusions have been removed from his mind, he will attain the highest Brahmic state and will then perform his daily duties, as we are now doing."

Ram came and paid his respect to all. Although his father, the King, tried to persuade him to sit on the throne with him, he refused and sat quietly among the crowd.

Raja Rishi Viswamitra then said to Ram: "O Brave Enemy of Sensual Objects, why are you drowning yourself in the Ocean of Delusion, which is only fit for the Ajnani (ignorant)? If you will tell us the cause of your suffering, then you will be relieved of it; you will then be able to attain that for which you are longing. Therefore, I beseech you to speak to us the truth."

Ram answered: "O Great Rishi, embodiment of Grace, you have allowed me to tell the cause of my suffering, and I beseech you to please listen to my story. I was born in my father's palace, studied and attained an education and gained much knowledge. I have journeyed around the earth visiting all Holy and Sacred places. When I returned from this pilgrimage, I found that my desires for this Universe had ceased; that life was full of delusion, without an iota of bliss within it. This world is an illusion from birth to death, and from death to birth. The worldly things are nothing except seeds of all unhappiness (pains). What is wealth or a kingdom? If we are seeking happiness, we find all unreal except Atma. When I try to learn what generates all worldly things, then I have no love for any of it. It is like the traveler who, when he has learned of the

3

unreality of the wave of the mirage in the desert, does not crave it. I am trying to set myself free of the sensual fire, but I am burning within like the old tree which has burned within by heat generated by itself. The load of delusion is pressing me down. I cannot bear it longer. I have tried to please my relatives, that they may not condemn me for my grief, but I cannot find a way out of it, though I have cried from the house-top.

The Wealth: "Wealth causes the mind of men to roam—seeking joy but bringing dangers. I have not seen anyone whose mind does not melt like snow, at the sight of wealth. This wealth not only destroys peace and joy which arises from spiritual wisdom, but it also produces hate, dishonesty, envy, jealousy and the like. All people, whether rich or poor, wise or foolish, peaceful or warlike, bow down to the degrading wealth. It causes people to be unjust, although it is useless as a flower under the hood of a Cobra.

The Prana: "The Prana (vital force) is like water pouring from a jar: it is going out of the body with the five senses; it is cutting short the lives of the ignorant. I am not enjoying this life of mine as my body is unreal. It is easy to control the ether, the winds, the waves of the ocean that rise and fall, but it is hard to control Prana. This body is not permanent. It is like winter cold and summer heat——it comes and goes. If we try to find its fruits, we only find bitter disappointments and sorrows . The life most worthwhile is that of those who have attained the highest Atmic wisdom, blessed with liberation, and freed from sorrows and pains. Life is worthwhile only to those who have freed themselves from rebirth. Others are only lives of folly—lives of the foolish. People without the power of discrimination, find that learning is only a burden to them. The person without peace of mind, finds that his mind is only a burden to him. The person who is full of passion, finds that the Atmic wisdom is only a burden to him. The person who has not found the blissful joy within himself finds that the body, the mind, the egoism and the actions are only burdens to him. Prana stays awhile in the body but often departs when the person is young, like the wise who do not stay in the company of the wicked.

The Egoism: "I am terrified by this harmful enemy of mine, egoism, which was born by illusion. It is the mother of many dangers. There is no worse danger than that of egoism. I fear this egoism will not leave me, as I have had to contend with it for a long time. I do not eat food with water. What is the use to speak of the other enjoyments? Doing anything through egoism is unreal. The sooner this egoism is given up, the better. As long as we tolerate egoism, just so long are desires created within us. I have given up all active thoughts that I may be free from egoism, but unhappiness is still clinging to me. I have not realized my own self. May you, O Rishi, be kind enough to bless me, that I may liberate myself of this enemy, egoism, which is the mother of all dangers in the universe. Its home is in the mind. It is false in its nature and is without intelligence or discrimination.

The Mind: "My mind is flying to sensual objects, resistless as though drawn by a magnet. This baneful mind does not like the real joy that comes from within, but travels outward to worldly pleasures. It is like a torrent, seething, writhing, uncontrolled, destroying in its onward rush, all the finer sensibilities. As a straw is tossed into the air, and a tree is shaken by the wind, so is the action of the mind. It lifts me up to the highest realm, then drops me unmercifully to the lowest depths of the earth. This terrible state of mind is more dangerous than a consuming flame. It is possible to dry up the ocean, to root out the Himalaya Mountains, or to eat fire, but it is harder, by far, to control the mind. It is the creator of all objects. This universe appeared when the mind came into existence, then disappeared with the absence of mind. Hence the mind should be controlled. With the control of mind, all pains and all sorrows will perish.

The Desires: "The desires, like owls of the air (anger, passion, etc.), fly into the sky of the Atma. During the night's slumber, these restless desires are mingled with the gloom of delusion. All my longing for good works is defeated by my desires. Without a spiritual mind, I am caught by desires, like a bird in a trap. The fire of my desires is burning me up, and I think that even a bath in ambrosia will not cool me. This owl of desires stirs up vain hopes within a person to strive for wealth, to attain- joy, or likes an old woman who dances for remuneration, rather than the joy of dancing. Likewise, all my desires try to roach for that which is impossible, because it is within. Desires, like monkeys, roam about without any place in view, passing over objects of desire, then longing for them again. It is these desires which bring the disease of re-birth—the worst of all diseases. This disease of desire can reach into well guarded forts. It is such desires as these that make the inner man manifest outwardly, like the rays of sunshine which cause the lotus buds to burst into blossom. These desires of the mind are like a two edged sword or like a red hot iron which consumes the greatest of men into nothingness.

"The body is made of five elements which vary in form—some lean and others fat. It is a house of ill, oscillating between pleasures and pains. What good can be gained through this body, except joys and sorrows? It is the house of egoism. The owner of the house has ten mischievous monkeys (the organs). The servant of this house is the mind which produces thoughts. If this body should exist forever, then it would be worthy of the longing, but it will perish at the sight of death. What is this body? It Is a composition of blood, tissues, and bones. It is subject to diseases and decay, and alike it serves for the poor, and for the rich. He, who believes in the illusory as the real, will cling to the body in delusion.

Childhood: "Anyone who is born in the ocean of the universe will keep rolling to and fro with its waves. Childhood is possessed of dangers, helplessness, and is unable to express thoughts, ideas, etc.. This stage of life is so filled with fears incurred by the parents, relatives, and elders, that none can enjoy it.

Youth: "The fearful and helpless time rolls out to the. next dangerous step as youth, when he receives hard blows dealt by the devil known as, The God of Love, whose hiding place is in the mind. The broadening of his view, the achievements of knowledge, the help of the teacher, and all good works, could not save the youth when he falls blindly into the pit of the sensual, or is caught by the Hunter known as The God of Love. The pleasures of youth increase until he finds that the youthful period is over; that he is only a man who has attained Nirvana while in the youthful age. Such a man is fit to be worshipped. Is there any period in the life of man which is safe from surrounding dangers? Yes, if we find a tree in the sky above.

The Lusts: "There are lusts for women, gold and wine. When man has indulged in any of the above lusts, then his body and mind burns without fuel, so that it produces heat. Men are caught through greediness for these lusts, as fish are caught with bait. If the lust for the above ceases, then men are free from all worldly bondage, which has its seat in the mind. Without giving up lust there is no chance of obtaining the Brahmic state, which is the highest state of existence.

The Old Age: "The time of childhood is past, the youth is spent, and now the worst time of all, that of old age must step into reign. If it arrives in company with disease and sorrow, then the Atma will bid it adieu. Like the love which ceases for the old wife when the husband finds a new mate, so the Atma gives up the old body full of diseases, for the new one. In old age, one suffers more and more as he has no power to gratify his desires. He is helpless to accomplish his desires, and quivers with old age while those about are laughing at him. If he happens to possess yellow dust (gold), then his children and relatives are praying for his death—that his gold may become theirs). Old age, which is beset with dangers and helplessness, is burning within and has no power to cope with the desires. The longing for various lusts will increase with old age but the power to gratify the thirst for more will leave. Day and night the fear of death seizes him from all sides. It is more difficult to control the desires in old age, for they have increased with the experiences of life.

The Time: "As all pains arise through ignorance, so is the end of life at the sight of death, which comes to all. As certain as fish die without water, so sure is death to the rich and the poor, to the powerful and to the weak. The forest, the mountains, the whole universe will die at its given time, and the whole will be born again after that time (the cycle) is over.

The Sakti (Power): "This destructive Sakti puts an end to all things. It melts this universe to nothingness and draws the whole to it for a time. There is no one who can withstand its victorious bow and near its arrows, for this great Sakti is superior to them all. Its head is the Heaven, its feet are the Hells, its body is the earth, its eyes are the sun and the moon, etc. Sometimes it takes the form of Rudra, another time it is Vishnu, another time it becomes Brahma, and during the Pralaya it took the shape of a terrific Bhairava. All these things or objects which I have described, are not real, but have arisen through egoism and the mind. I do not know the object or aim of this birth or the reason for the disease of desires within the heart of every being. It is very hard to find one who has freed himself from the diseases of desires, but a great spiritual enlightenment is gained through the contact with such a one. The wise are few and for that reason the means of liberation are not known. The mind which is deluded by illusion lacks the kindness of heart, has no compassion for good and is indifferent to good or bad. When it realizes what is good, then cowardice is replaced by courage; this world by Heaven. It is seldom we meet the blessed one whose mind is controlled, but we meet the ignorant often. All baneful thoughts produce bondage. All desires and egos will leave the body and go to the Heavens or other worlds or planets. All countries will change, all mountains become dust, all three worlds will perish, the oceans, the stars, the sun, the people, with or without power, the Trinity (Brahma—Creator, Vishnu—Preserver and Rudra—Destroyer) will be absorbed up to the highest reality. Brahma who creates by His will and along with its law, comes to an end; all the Akasa (space) and the Macrocosm merge into the Parameshwara (non-dual; Supreme God), that which is the liberator from the delusion of illusions . This reality, above thought or speech, is pure wisdom. People are always anxious to engage in such thoughts as: 'This is the time for good works.' 'When will be a good time to visit the Holy Places?' 'Relatives are a great help.' 'I cannot do as I used to do.' 'I cannot enjoy the things that I once enjoyed.' These people want to follow the Great One, but are too engrossed in home, wife, comforts of life, and obtaining wealth. They are always between the two. When a child is born, they are happy; when death claims another, they are grieved. Should one succeed in obtaining a great amount of wealth he is called the King of Riches. But behold! There comes death who puts an end to all!

"Lead me to the path by which I shall be free from all delusions. Surrounded by great danger, the brave hero dies at the hands of a coward. Hundreds of people die at the mercy of a man. This is the play of Sakti. My mind is burned by earthly fire. I have no desire for wealth. I prefer death to the pleasures of life. I prefer to live without sorrow and disappointments, but I find it impossible to free my mind. If you, with your well controlled mind, will not remove my grief, then to whom shall I go? The dangers of poison are not poisonous to me, but the sensual objects are my woe. The former kills only the body, but the latter ruins many bodies of future birth. Free from objects of love or hate, the sages, like you, with quietness of mind are ever engaged in seedless Samadhi (highest meditation state). My mind is indifferent toward the material or the spiritual. Please show me the way to bliss that is above pain or pleasure, doubt or delusion. That eternal state can't be reached by the five senses. I desire the path by which the Great Righteous ones manage to escape from the sufferings of this world. Please be kind enough to tell me—is there not a higher state of existence? Is there not a state of quietness? If there is no one who will unlock that door for me, then may I not attain that peaceful state by my own efforts alone? I am without doubt and egoism, I do not care for food, water, nor fine clothes. I will not perform my daily duties. I do not care to read scriptures, nor do I care for pleasures or pains. Above love and hate, I shall always be silent and desireless."

Thus Ram ended his story of misery and darkness and asked for light.

Two

HOW SUKA ATTAINED HIGHEST STATE OF BLISS

After hearing the story of Ram concerning the Universe and its miseries, everyone in the assembly hall were not only pleased but the Sidhas showered flowers and spoke words of praise: "O Ram, your utterances are full of wisdom. It is very difficult to drive joy from this world, for though it was created for Devas, who were full of joy, it is now full of suffering and pain. If Ram's indifference toward the world is true. O Rishi, then we may be justified with what we are doing. If we, the Sidhas and Rishis, love the things or objects which Ram hated, we should perhaps be classed with the ignorant."

Raja Rishi Viswamitra said to Ram: "You know all that should be known. You and Rishi Suka are full of spiritual wisdom. Both of you have attained equally the highest wisdom, but you need to acquire the state of quietness and stillness."

Ram: "O, please inform me how Brahm Rishi Suka achieved wisdom without quiescence of mind, and how he secured that blissful state?"

The Teacher: "Rishi Suka had absolute spiritual wisdom which is the only sword to cut the rope of re-birth. Once he tried to inquire of the origin of things, as you are doing, and he then became doubtful of his wisdom. The object of his mind became disturbed, but he was free from sensual desires. Rishi Suka went to the Himalaya Mountains to his father, who was one of the Masters there, and asked for instruction so that he might not lose his faith. Thus he said to his father: 'O Father, from whence came all this Maya (illusion), which produces misery and darkness? How did it originate? How may it be destroyed?' What part does it play in the origin of the universe?' His father replied with wisdom, as he did unto all others, but his answer did not dispel his son's doubt. Suka said to his father: 'I know all that.' Alas, his father was unable to remove his doubt. His father then requested him to go to King Janak, who was the highest being in spiritual wisdom of his time.

"Rishi Suka left the Himalaya Mountains and later approached the golden gates of the King's palace. Although the King was aware of Rishi Suka's arrival, he refused to go forth and meet him. He requested that the Rishi should not be admitted into his palace, as he wanted to test the sincerity of his mind. Rishi Suka waited for seven days at the golden gate. At last he was conducted into a magnificent hall where beautiful women were indulging in worldly enjoyments. But Suka's mind did not lose its balance. He was not affected by the unjust act of the King in making him wait seven days at his gate, nor was he moved by the disgraceful conduct of worldly association. The King came and addressed him thus: 'O, Brahm Rishi (there are three kinds of Rishis), you have reached the highest state. The worldly joys and sorrows do not affect you. I beseech you to tell me what brought you here?' Rishi Suka asked: 'What has caused my illusion? How does it generate? How can it be destroyed? Please instruct me.' The King gave him the same explanation that his father had given him. Rishi Suka returned: 'I know that, and my father gave me the same information. If Maya produced by a differentiation of one Atma such as as breath and merged again into the Atma, then no benefit can be derived from this perishable Maya . O Highest Guru, you are able to dispel this delusion of my mind! Please enlighten me on this matter.'

"The King: 'You have known what should be known, but still you ask me—although your father has instructed you aright. The enlightenment we have given to you is the real one. Atma alone, is that which is everywhere, just as the ether pervades all space and atmosphere. Wisdom is bound by naught else but its own thought. Freeing yourself from sensual thoughts is freeing yourself from bondage. You have clearly realized the Atmic wisdom for you have given up all longing for sensual objects. you have by thine own efforts, through the higher mind, reached the highest Brahmic State; you have become a Jivanmukta (the state of emancipated embodiment). But one thing you have yet to accomplish—that of giving up the delusion of the illusion which has arisen through doubt in your mind. When you have accomplished this, then you will be free.' King Janak thus initiated Rishi Suka into the Atmic mysteries, where he acquired the highest state of wisdom and was freed from all misery, doubt, death and rebirth. He lived for 1000 years, then merged into that higher wisdom, which is Brahm. As water returns to the ocean, so the light which departs from the "I", returns to the higher light (Atma), and becomes Brahm. Thus Rishi attained that liberation, which is above all else. O Ram, you should follow the same path.

"To become a slave of desire is bondage; to master it, is liberation. Master your desires and become indifferent to worldly enjoyments; become a Jivanmukta, without the assistance of austerities of religions; follow the path of wisdom and you will realize the reality. O Ram, there is but one person who can remove the doubt from your mind, and that is the Omniscient Vashisht, who knows the past, present, and the future. He is the Guru of all mankind."

Rishi Viswamitra turned toward Rishi Vashisht and suggested that he should be taught the stories of Brahmic Wisdom, since he is qualified for such instruction. The Brahmic Wisdom should be given only to those who have complete control of themselves and withheld from those who doubt and are full of vice. Thus Viswamitra ends the story of Suka. The Munis and Rishis, who were present in the assembly hall, praised Rishi Viswamitra's noble instruction.

Rishi Vashisht said: "O Muni, I shall do according to your request. I shall relate the stories of pure wisdom, which have been given out by Brahma, that mankind may be liberated from the chain of rebirth."

Three

THE WAY TO BLESSED LIBERATION

Rishi Vashisht: "Now, O Ram, listen to me. Try to follow the Sastaric (right path). The goal of mankind can be achieved in this life, which is reached by means of two paths. One is by the way of Atmic Wisdom; the other, by the ordinary path, which leads to liberation (death). Virtuous people will attain liberation by following the Atmic Wisdom and through the association with the Wise, thus developing high qualities."

Ram: "I am under control of desires, which I have made in my past lives. My efforts have not been in the right direction. O Teacher, what am I to do?"

Rishi Vashisht: "O Ram, by one's own efforts alone, can the Brahmic or Divine state be achieved, and by none else. Desires can be classed under two divisions: that of pure and impure.

These desires will cling to future births. If the impure desires are upper-most in one's life then misery is experienced by its future lives. In case that pure desires prevail, then liberation is easily acquired. O Ram, with all your power, cultivate the Brahmic science. Free yourself of impure desires and retain the pure. See all things with equal vision and strive to bar that door of the mind from whence cometh the impure desires; but open all other doors through which cometh the pure desires. Cast out all impure desires and generate the pure ones. If doubt arises as to where these pure desires shall lead, you shouldst continue to hold them, as no bad can come from them until your mind has realized the Reality of Brahm. Always follow the path of Brahm by Veda (the Sacred Knowledge). Let Guru initiate you into Brahm. O Ram, may you remain immovable in the study of Realization. Free your mind of impure desires and with pure desires attain the Atmic state which is free of all pain and suffering. Kill all your illusory thoughts so that they may never be resurrected again. Develop peace of mind and bliss within yourself. Free yourself of worldly desires and become One with Brahm. Try to understand the significance of the Holy sentence, "Tat Twamasi" (you are that), and meditate upon the Reality.

Rishi Vashisht's Own Story: "Now listen to Brahm's utterances. Out of the highest Chidakasa (highest ether) or wisdom which is all pervading and is the seat or root of all objects, arose Brahm. Vishnu, the earth, and all other objects rose from his heart. Brahm found that many worthy souls were suffering in Bharatavarsa. He was moved by pity for the liberation of these souls. He concluded that the cycle of birth or death could not be controlled by Japa Chanting (Chanting of Mantras), Tapas (religious austerities), visiting Holy places, or by bathing in the Holy Ganges: only through the Atmic Wisdom. By the power of his will, he created all mankind like unto himself. So, I was born and have paid my respects to him. I was given a seat on the North side of him. There he cured me of my illusion which had enveloped me for some time. All my wisdom had deserted me. My mind became confused and my actions were foolish, as are the actions of the ignorant. When I came out of this state of mind, He asked me the cause of my misery. In turn I asked him these questions: 'How did this universe arise? How may liberation be attained?' In answer to these questions, he blessed me with true liberation of highest state, through which I realized the highest Atmic Wisdom. He said, 'it was we, who put you under the influence of Maya and released you again. We have ordained that all souls shall be initiated by your wisdom in order to attain their liberation. you shall soon go to India which is the Land of Religions. You shall initiate those who are seeking wisdom into the Atmic Wisdom, but not those who are lovers of egoism.'

"Accordingly I came to India and will live here as long as humanity exists. I have no worldly desires, consequently, I will escape that dreamless sleep state of existence. I have overcome that mental pain and misery, which is experienced daily throughout the world. O Ram, only those who prefer the Atmic Wisdom to the material knowledge will know the Atma (self).

"There are four soldiers who guard the road to liberation. They are Patience (or peace of mind), Atmic Inquiry, Contentment, and Association with the Wise. If you can succeed in making one of the above a friend, then the others will be easy. That one will introduce you to the others. Without gaining their friendship, they will not permit you to enter upon the road to liberation. So by all means, gain the friendship of one of the above and start on the road to liberation, for without liberation there is no end to rebirths. Association with the Wise will mean to you, what Garuda Mantra means to the persons who have been bitten by the Cobra. Once that wisdom is attained then that person is safe, no harm can come to that person. No one can achieve that blissful state by merely inquiring about the Atmic Wisdom. It must come through self experience or through the help of a Guru. Merely reading books of wisdom breeds more ignorance. Keep in mind that it will be much better to live by begging for food from the outcasts, than to live an ignorant life. O Ram, if only one of the four guards is made your friend—namely, Patience is mastered—then all your miseries and sorrows will fly from you as darkness flies from the light. Those who have mastered patience will never be upset by poverty or wealth. They will remain the same in peace or war. They will not make a distinction between birth and death. These noble people will be higher than the man of mere knowledge, and will surely attain liberation. May you, O Ram, attain patience! If Atmic Inquiry along with patience should be developed, then surely the state of the highest wisdom will be acquired. This Atmic-inquiry enables one to understand cause and effect, which is the seed of rebirth. One must rid themselves of all doubt by the power of discrimination, which is always a shining light. One should always inquire: 'From where did I come?' 'From where did the universe come?' Such inquiries dispel that dark cloud of ignorance.

"Contentment is the Noble who will set us free of all grief, for such arises only from the sensual objects of desire. One who has mastered noble contentment will always be happy. His mind will ever seek the Atmic Wisdom. Persons of contentment will ever be worshipped by all mankind.

"Association with the Wise will help us to overcome the Maya. It is not the bathing in the waters of the Holy Ganges, that is so helpful to the thousands that throng there each year, but the associations with the wise are more helpful to self realization than making gifts, sacrifices, etc.. The Wise are like ships that help us safely across the ocean of rebirths. These four roads are the ways and means to bliss. O Ram, listen to these stories. They are light, which dispel the delusion of Maya. Understand the inner meaning and search deeply for the Atmic Wisdom. All delusion will perish, and the mind will become calm and peaceful like the waters of a lake. Such persons will not suffer the disappointments of life. They will not be affected by the storm of Maya. They will have balance of mind as steady as the Himalaya Mountains. The truth seeker who will follow this path of Atmic Wisdom will always find enjoyment in Samadhi. This is the way to Jivanmukta. He is desireless, and nothing is supernatural to him. Words cannot describe this state of mind. He will move in this universe like all others, but his mind is free from the bondage of earthly desires. Good and bad cannot affect him. He will be recognized by others as the happiest. He will not interfere with the paths of others, but always follow the path of Atmic Wisdom. After he has reached this attainment, he will never be born again. He is worthy of all his accomplishments, while others may not be worthy even of their human birth. He should perform his duties of life earnestly, through earning and spending correctly. He should ever seek to reach this fourth state of existence through the Atmic inquiry, keeping his well balanced mind alert, for this state is obtained only through Atmic inquiry.

"He who attains the fourth state is above thought. If he is the Master of Quietness, he will surely gain liberation whether he lives with his family or alone; whether he is performing the daily duties of everyday life or not, he will be one with the Reality. Follow this path and many analogies will be given out in order that Brahmic wisdom may be realized within you, as all have their purpose and aim in the One principle. The ignorant say that pure wisdom is not subject to analogies. Mixing of name and form should not be made subject of this inquiry. Such an absurd argument is not worthy, for Wisdom is obtained by the Atmic inquiry. O Ram, you should not let your mind accept thoughts of doubt. Always remember these four: Patience, Atmic Inquiry, Contentment and Association with the Wise. These four guard the gate of liberation. No one can secure liberation until his friendship with the four is developed. This is the road to the attainment of bliss. By attention to the following stories, you will surely attain wealth of Atmic Wisdom and a happy life."

Four

CREATION OF THE UNIVERSE

And the Rishi Vashisht, preceptor of the Divine Ram, went on: "The poison plant of the world's illusion springs from the mind entangled in sensuous enjoyment. But it is through mind alone, that the ills of mind can be cured and eradicated. Those who live in this world without attachment to worldly objects, like a duck in a pond, are the true conquerors of the mind. For what are they—but vermin—those who cling to the objects of the senses, and taste not of the fruit of renunciation? One ought to rid the mind of all thoughts of ego, and fix it on the Soul Supreme, according to the teachings of the Vedas (Four books of Wisdom), to attain complete bliss and harmony in life.

"Even as one thorn removes another thorn, so the higher mind of a man, will remove the impurities from the lower mind of man. To cleanse the mind of its defilements and desires is the first step on the high road to salvation, trodden by the great

Saint and Sages.

"When the mind that wavers and flickers like a flame in the wind, is steadied and made one-pointed, as it were, through desirelessness, then alone is the Real Truth that sustains the Universe made manifest in all its refulgent majesty. May you tread this Sacred and Ancient Path (Yoga), O Ram, and by knowing the true nature of your own self, and freeing your mind from all worldly entanglements, attain to the highest bliss of salvation. May your mind, freed from hankerings and longings for the objects of the world, be merged in God-Consciousness. Past, present and future become as one, to he who has controlled his mind, and conquered his worldly desires. When all the shining tinsel of the world becomes a mere nothing. then alone is mind conquered. These thoughts of attachment and possession,—that this is mine, that is thine, etc., belong to the realm of the lower mind. When all such lower thoughts of differentiation are lost, and the Atma, One behind all, is recognized, then alone the sorrows of the world cease to exist. May you, O Ram, attain that Divine State. When the mind is fully controlled and the desires arising from it are destroyed, then alone comes surcease from pains and afflictions that torment humanity. When the baser passions of the mind are slain, then one attains perfect peace, and becomes, as it were the fountainhead of peace in the world for the salvation of suffering humanity.

"By meditating on the heart, spiritual Wisdom awakens, all doubts vanish, and the mind is contented. This mind of ours, is susceptible to all kinds of influences, hankering after worldly pleasures, and this is the greatest obstacle in the path of salvation. Control your. mind with the thought that these worldly objects are the merest tinsel compared to the liberation which is a veritable treasure-trove of all bliss and happiness. Then will you be freed from all worldly thoughts of possession and differentiation, arising from an overgrown ego. The Divine State of liberation, where one is freed from the cycle of birth and death, confers untold bliss, and is everlasting like the Eternal One Himself.

"It is indeed hard to find in this world, a mind really free from the snare of the senses. To control this ever-fluctuating mind and make it one-pointed is the aim of all meditation, and is the theme of all discourses on metaphysics. Constant meditation on the One Unchanging Reality of the Universe, which is God, the Self Supreme. The mind takes on the qualities it meditates upon. For that reason the wise keep within strict control, those tendencies of the mind which incline it toward the baser objects, and in the end attain the Bliss of complete freedom, liberation, or Nirvana.

"The moment desires and distractions crop up in the mind, they should be weeded out. The destruction of sensuous desires is akin to the destruction of ignorance. Desirelessness leads to the peace of salvation. Constant effort is necessary to attain such bliss. With the realization of the Supreme and Sustaining Reality of the Universe, one sees that all worldly objects are false and unreal to the core,—mere illusions, nothing else, like bubbles on the deep."

Prince Ram asked: "Tell us, O Guru, how one can destroy ignorance?"

Rishi Vashisht replied: "Through ignorance it is, O Ram, that the Atma, which is eternal, is forced to go through the cycle of births and deaths. To conceive of the illusion, which besets the embodied soul as real, is ignorance, and a barrier to seeing true reality. A man, free from births and deaths, and realizing the all-refulgent reality of the Universe, perceives that desires are a creation of Maya. Extinction of lower desires is the extinction of ignorance."

Prince Ram asked his preceptor, Rishi Vashisht: "All visible objects of name and form, O Lord, you say are illusions, and that illusion is destroyed by meditation on the true reality of the Atma. Pray, what is this thing called Atma?"

Rishi Vashisht replied: "It is the Wisdom of the Brahma, who has no visible form. All things of the world, perceived through our senses, contain the essence of Brahma, such as growth, mind, birth and death, which are illusory, not real. Brahma alone is true and self-existent, the Creator and Upholder of the Universe. Out of that Supreme Soul, which is Eternal, Immortal, and Absolute, arose the intelligence that governs the Universe. This Atmic Jnan is the Absolute Self shining everywhere.

"From the Brahma arise different forces and powers like waves and currents in the ocean. To realize Oneself as Brahma is the goal; but to know the soul as distinct from the body is to know the truth and be free from ignorance. It is only the fancy of fools, that gives illusion the garb of reality. The wise have pierced the veil of illusion by the shafts of their Jnan (Wisdom). Know then, this body, this wealth, these kith and kin are not real. Atma alone is real and eternal. Perform actions in this world without being absorbed by them."

Sri Ram then said: "How marvelous it is an illusion, which is unreal, should cause so much pain and suffering in the world, and that which appears so solid and concrete should be but a manifestation of Maya. O Teacher, I cannot believe this Universe really came out of the unreality. How do you account for the pains of King Lavana?"

Rishi Vashisht answered: "King Lavana was not bound by the results of his actions, as he performed them without attachment, and with complete indifference to the outcome. One morning while sitting in solitude, the King fell into a profound reverie and thought of performing mentally the Raj-suya Vajna, as performed by his powerful ancestor Harish Chandra. He thought of all the accessories to the Sacrifice, and in imagination offered oblations to the gods, and went through all the details of the sacrifice. When he awoke from his reverie, it was night-fall. It is a rule that whoever performs the Royal Sacrifice, must undergo great pain and suffering. So the King of the gods, Indra, sent a celestial messenger to inflict suffering on King Lavana. The mendicant, who appeared before the King, and put him into a trance in which he suffered cruelly, was none other than Indra's messenger. This I discovered by my ascetic powers. So you will see from this episode that actions performed even mentally have far-reaching consequences.

"The story of King Lavana is as follows: A mendicant came to the Court of King Lavana and besought him to witness his powers. With the King's consent, the mendicant waved a peacock feather before the King's face, and immediately the King sank into unconsciousness, while his body writhed fearfully. When some time later the King recovered consciousness, his minister asked him what he had experienced. The King replied: 'I felt dizzy when the mendicant waved the fan. Then I saw a horse coming toward me. On the mendicant's suggestion I rode the horse and was carried away to a dense forest, where I fell from the horse and felt very thirsty. While I lay dying of thirst, I saw a young woman pass my way with a pitcher of water. I asked for water, but the girl refused, saying that she was low-born and could not give water to the King unless he married her and promised to live with her folks. In my extremity, I consented. I married the girl, but found it very hard to live with her folks, who were no better than barbarians. I moved up on the hill top and built a house. There I lived with the girl for eight years, and we had two sons. Then there was a severe drought that led to terrible famine. People died by the hundreds and thousands for want of food. I started, with my wife and sons, for some other land. On the way, my wife died from fatigue and exhaustion and my sons cried for food. Unable to see them suffer, I killed myself. Just at this point I recovered consciousness.' So said the King, and all present marvelled at the strangeness of the dream. They looked around for the ascetic but he was nowhere to be found."

"O Ram," continued the Rishi Vashisht, "I will speak to you of the nature of Jnan and Ajnana—Wisdom and Ignorance. Each of these is seven-fold in character. Wisdom enables men to perceive the true reality of the Universe and thereby obtain salvation; whereas, ignorance, by regarding the physical body as the real 'I', leads to bondage.

"Now, the difference between a seer and one who is denied

spiritual vision. The seers are those who have conquered illusions, and have awakened to a realization of the true reality of the Universe. The ignorant slaves of illusion. Shallow human intelligence causes doubts and disbeliefs and leads men astray. This is but delusion. Wisdom leaves no room for doubts or disbelieves. To the man who has attained true Wisdom, the human soul and the Supreme Soul becomes One.

"The seven states of ignorance are Bindu-jagrat, Jagrat, Maha-jagrat, Swapnajagrat, Swapuna, Sushupti, Bindu-jagrat is the primary state of partial perception. In the second state the individual begins to perceive the difference of mine, thine and his. In the third state the man begins to have some conception of the relationship between man and the Universe. In the fourth state the mind realizes its supremacy over matter. The fifth state is really the dream state. In the sixth state the individual recalls to mind things long past. In the seventh state the individual realizes the futility of all his previous states, fraught with pain and suffering.

"There are likewise seven states of Wisdom, although any number of divisions and subdivisions can be made. These seven states of Wisdom lead to Nirvana. They are Subeccha or right desire, Vicharan or contemplation, Tanumansi, the state in which the mind is alert, Satwapatti or the generation of the serenity of the mind, Asansakti or detachment of the mind from worldly things, Padarth Bhavana, the perception of the truth and reality, and Turya or light. These states free the seeker from delusion and lead gradually to complete Nirvana or salvation and to the end of pain and suffering. Subhecha or right desire is of course the longing and desire for spiritual enlightenment.

Vicharana is defined as meditation or contemplation of the things of spirit and mind, contemplation of the Divinity that pervades the Universe, and the realization of the Godhead. These two states lead to the third stage of keen intellectual perception, which naturally leads to the real truth or divine philosophy. Atma Jnan (Wisdom of the self) brings about emancipation from the thraldom of worldly things. This state confers ineffable bliss and enlightenment on the seeker. By logical sequence in that state of advancement, the student realizes his relationship with the Divine, and his relationship with the Universe. here he sees, knows and understands all. Then the last state of complete enlightenment and mastery is reached, when the very presence of the man radiates spiritual light. Such a soul is free from the cycle of birth and death. He is called Jivanmukta. These souls are free indeed. Free front worldly longings and desires, pleasure, pair, success, failure, praise, blame, profit, loss, victory and defeat are as one to them. They have attained salvation by the continued discipline of their mind, by unceasing effort in the realm of divine philosophy.

"Rising by degrees from one spiritual stage of enlightenment to another, until having passed through the seven stages, you attain liberation. Those who have subjected their mind and acquired true perception of the Divine within, are truly great, worthy of every respect, and adoration. Others have to go through innumerable births and deaths. One desire leads to another. Thus the wheels of Maya move on, and the soul is bound more and more, until true awakening comes, and the man starts on the path of enlightenment. This path begins with the desire for spiritual light and attains completion with acquirement of that light by means of the seven stages described above. Such a one realizes Brahma and becomes one with Brahma, the first Cause of the Universe, the Source of Ineffable Bliss, the Ocean of Power, the Sun of Spiritual Illumination, Immortal, Untreated, All-pervading, All-seeing, All-knowing, All-powerful, Supreme Creator, Preserver and Destroyer of the Universe."

Rishi Vashisht continued: "O Ram, I will narrate further the story of King Lavana to illustrate the working of the Maya. On recovering consciousness, the King was seized with a great longing to visit the strange country he had dreamed of, so he started for the Vindhya mountains and in due time reached the impenetrable forest that covered its slopes.

"He wandered about hither and thither until he reached the North, where he came upon a settlement of the very people he had dreamed about. And wonder of wonders, these people were actually suffering from famine and in a miserable plight. The King and his courtiers saw an old woman bewailing the loss of her children, who had died during the famine. As they listened to her lament, they discovered with much surprise that the old woman was weeping for the girl whom the King had married in his dream, by whom he had two sons, and who had died while on the way to a land of plenty. Greatly moved by the incident, the King pacified the old woman, giving her and her tribesmen food and clothing and conducting them to his kingdom. He then sought an explanation of the mystery, at the feet of the learned. After due discipline, meditation, and study he attained the Bliss of Nirvana. It is thus, O Ram, that illusion works and gives the unreal, the appearance of the real."

Ram asked: "How was it, O Teacher, that what the King saw in his dream actually came to pass?"

Rishi Vashisht replied: "You will better understand this incident by the story of Gandhi, which I will narrate for your benefit later on. What happened in this case was not really true, only a conjurer's trick played by Indra's messenger on the consciousness of the King and those aborigines on the Vindhya Mountains. The King experienced in his unconscious state, and the tribesmen saw in their conscious state, that was all. But that is how illusion works, tricking us into believing as real that which is not, piercing the veil of illusion, O Ram, by the shining shaft of Jnan. May you attain that state of bliss, my son, in which the human soul becomes one with the Divine—the state of complete Nirvana. May you realize the Divinity within you, and know it to be the same that brought the world into being and pervades and sustains it. Conquer, O Ram, by ceaseless meditation, the ignorance of illusion, and attain the One Omnipotent and Omniscient God, from whom the world evolved, and in whom it resolves itself."

Five

QUEEN CHUNDALAI, THE GREAT YOGIN

"O may you rest yourself in your all peaceful Atma like the King Sikhithwaya who controlled the restless bird called Mind," said Rishi Vashisht to Ram.

Whereupon Ram asked him: "Tell me, O Guru, who was the King Sikhithwaya, possessor of the peaceful Bliss? Let me learn how may Jnana, which is the basis of everything, arise in me to its fullest power."

The Rishi Vashisht replied: "King Sikhithwaya was born in the Dwapara Yuga. Over his people he ruled wisely and well. His justice had no bond by-ways. He had but one purpose—to do good and perform the works of virtue. Master over body and mind, his great joy lay in the happiness of his Subjects.

"Chundalai, his Queenly Consort, born through Tapas, to the Queen of the Sourashtra country was like a peacock in beauty. Her beauty glowed like a jewel in the perfect setting of her sterling virtue.

"This King and Queen lived together in perfect happiness, fulfilling their duties without the slightest difference of opinion. Their youth passed delightfully, united in body and mind, and their days flowed away like water from a broken jar, and middle age hovered over them like clouds on a rainy day. They had tasted the passion fruit of worldly things. In their youth they loved this and desired that, but now materiality fell from them like a worn-out garment: The only desire left was to obtain Atma-Jnana (Wisdom of the self), for this wisdom is the only certain ending of the disease of rebirth.

"Realizing there is no escape from the disease of rebirth, except through Atma-Jnan, they started toward the attainment of this goal with minds fixed in true meditation. About them were gathered the Wise and Learned of their time. In this environment of Harmony and Peace, they collected a store of Wisdom, and led a truly spiritual life.

"Queen Chundalai, she of true discernment, having heard and understood well the real significance of the Sastra (Scripture) taught by the Wise, for the attainment of the Higher spirituality, said to herself—since there exists Atma as I fully realize, why do we use the term 'I'? From whence comes this illusion to the mind; to what is it due; how does it arise? The body is not the 'I', as the body is visible to us, and is changeable and incomplete in itself. Nor can it designate the organs functioning in the body, nor its moving force Prana. Further, it does not describe the mind which owes its activity to thought. The term Jiva cannot be applied to the 'I', as the Jiva is the individual soul. I have learned through this enquiry that Atma-jnana will never be attained through the senses, but through the Eternal Jnana. I know my Jiva exists through Atmic reality. This Atmic Wisdom becomes known only by knowing oneself, not through another. This self-wisdom or self light shines everywhere.

"By divine realization the Queen enjoyed the consciousness of the reality of the Atma self, and discharged her daily duties without desire for their fruits. Longing ceased, and the inclination of her mind toward the pairs of opposites, love and hate, cold and heat. She became the receptacle of Bliss as a result of the control of her mind. Then with the daily Yoga practices, the Queen developed Atmic reality, that true realization, which is a certainty beyond explanation. Only he knows it, who has realized the reality. The beautiful Queen shone with a radiant Spiritual Light.

"The King noted the refulgence of his wife's beauty with great pleasure. He asked his Queen, 'O Beloved One, you are now radiant with such great beauty, it is as if your youth had come back again, or as if you had sipped a divine nectar by which you have attained Eternal Divine beauty. You seem so happy, your mind so blessed with divine peace, that you are perfect in body and mind. Tell me, my Queen, of the wonderous purity which so dazzles me.'

"Queen Chundalai replied: 'Having abandoned and risen above this world which is form but formless, real but without reality,

34

I attained the Mighty One, who is the reality beyond the older age or death. Hence, the radiance in my body, which is but the reflection of the refulgent peace within. I have realized That God is the essential nature of all; being the atom of atoms; the whole without creation or destruction. That is why my body is radiant. I have no joy in the object of the senses, yet do I partake of the Bliss and happiness of beauty. Love and hate have both gone from me, and every hour I glory in the attainment of physical beauty and contentment, but the objects my eyes and mind behold awake no response in me, either of joy or sorrow. I have attained super-consciousness, which is the cause of my Bliss and beauty.'

"Hearing the explanation from his wife, the King, without understanding or trying to understand her words, said: 'O Beloved, you have given utterance to words which are not befitting you. Have you lost your mental balance? How is it that you, living in palaces and in the luxuries of wealth, should attain the realization of Atma when the greatest of men have cut themselves off from the outward world and have sought the quiet retreats of the Himalaya Mountains, in order to attain that state of Bliss, or Atma? How can a Queen, like you, realize that which can only be realised by the Wise? You may say that you have enjoyed that blessed state, like those who were unable to reach that exalted state, but claimed they had sensed it intuitively within. Tell me, how can you realise the Atma within? You who are a poor fragile creature, without Wisdom, tossed to and fro by the senses.'

"The Queen was touched by the King's remarks. She pitied the poor King, who had not reached that state in which he could understand or enjoy the Divine Bliss. Still the King and Queen lived together in Peace and Harmony as they had done in the past. The Queen had gained perfect control over her mind and desires. She thought if she were able to develop the power of levitation, then it would be easy to convince her King of her power. For this purpose she practised Madras in Yoga for the attainment of levitation."

Ram said to the Master: "Please explain how one may attain such psychic power as levitation."

The Master answered: "I am telling you the interesting story of the Queen, and now you should not ask for an explanation of Yoga. However, I will answer you. By control of Prana (Vital or Life Force), one may attain that power. One who wishes to attain that power should have a balanced diet, should practice Mudras and Postures. Control of the mind is also necessary as well as the study and ceaseless practice of Yoga. One should have the help of a Spiritual Teacher. One should be free from anger, love and hate. Try to understand the nature of Prana (Vital or Life Force) and control its movements, then you can Master the forces of nature, Sidhi (psychic), and attain liberation.

"There is in the midst of the one hundred Nadis (energy channel), one which is called Kundalini, it is within every being from Brahma to worm. It is like a serpent, and is sleeping as the serpent sleeps in the winter. When the Kundalini power is aroused, it enables one to master the powers of nature. All other Nadis of the body are connected with the Kundalini. The powers of the Kundalini become useful, through the

Light of Wisdom. This power, through meditation becomes meditation, through wisdom becomes wisdom, mind through mind, thought through thought, egoism through egoism.

"This greatest of all powers may easily be controlled, if one masters the Prana. The Prana always goes upward, the Apana, (or other vital force) always goes downward. These two vital or life forces cause death of the body. If Prana is brought down, and Apana is permitted to rise and mix in the heart, then disease would leave the body, never to return."

Ram again said to the Master: "Please explain how mental disease can be destroyed."

The Master answered: "Diseases which affect the mind are the first and are not the easiest to heal; those which affect the body may be classed as secondary. The desires which affect the mind are primary diseases; we have sunk this far by absence of Wisdom, and lack of Mastery over ourselves. We are under the seeming power of delusion. We cannot realise to what extent we are pulled down by such delusion. The mental disease is similar to the coming of a winter storm. When the power of desires gets hold of one, he then is liable to be guilty of fearful karma; this in turn produces bodily disease.

"Bodily disease is also brought on by overeating, living in unhealthy places, association with the wicked, impure desires, evil thoughts, etc. These mental or indirect diseases have a direct effect upon the body.

"Now I will explain how both forms of disease perish, O Ram.

The wise say that the mental diseases have two divisions, common and specific, the former affect this body only, but the latter tend to rebirth, also. The common diseases may be banished by correct eating and right thinking.

"When the mind is not in perfect harmony it may affect the blood and produce discord in any portion of the body. Mental discord will produce poison in the blood, and the poison will affect the nervous system. When the nervous system is affected, then Prana cannot follow its right path. When Prana does not follow its right path, then it cannot reach all parts of the body as it should, and thus many of the nerves may wither or die. If harmony is established in the mind, all else is easy and simple. When harmony is established in the mind, it will naturally follow that one will want to do good and read good books pertaining to truth. When peace is established in the mind, then Prana will follow its right course and all disease will vanish.

"The path of Yoga, by which one may master the power of the Kundalini, is through the practise of Pranayama, which causes the power of the Kundalini to arise, and then the holy becomes strong. By Pranayama the movement of Prana and Apana may be controlled; then the Yogin will be able to go up like a bird. The Prana is the cause, and when it is made to go up through the Sushumna, all kinds of psychic powers are attained, such as seeing, hearing and levitation."

Ram again questioned Rishi Vashisht: "How do such people become light and heavy, seemingly at will, and how do they gain control over the powers of nature?"

The Master replied: "Such powers are mastered only by one who has a consciousness of absolute purity, free from the worldly things. The self is the finest of the fine, which is not the Universe, neither its association with it. But through its own thoughts becomes an individual soul, and is known by the name Jiva (individual soul). This Jiva mingles with many things in the world, forgets its reality and thinks of the body as being real. When one has the last awakening or illumination and determines to know the Absolute Reality, then the gross and unreal vanish and the real nature comes to light, and is revealed or manifested. Through meditation the psychic powers are awakened and mastered. This is the truth revealed to those who have gained mastery through Yoga.

"Through Yoga means, the Queen mastered the psychic powers, and with it encircled the world, simply to convince her King. No one knew that the Queen possessed such marvelous power. That was one reason her King did not believe or gain the state of Bliss. For the King was as ignorant of her blessed power, as a child is ignorant of higher education. The King was without peace of mind, so this great Yogin did not try to raise the King to Atmic Wisdom."

Ram then said: "O Master, how can others hope to attain pure Wisdom when the great King failed, when his wife, the great Yogin, tried to help him realise the blessed Wisdom? Speak, O Teacher, and say which is the right means to attain the goal?"

Rishi Vashisht answered: "Faith in the word of the Guru is the way, but discipleship alone is the means of reaching Atmic Wisdom."

Ram said: "If the disciple alone is the means of reaching the Atmic Wisdom, then why should it be necessary to have faith in the word of the Guru?"

The Teacher explained: "A certain hunter, who lived in the mountains, lost a shell while walking along through the grassy forest; he was greatly worried about the lost shell and went searching for it. After a long search he came upon a gem shining like a moon. Searching for his shell led to the finding of a precious gem. Such may be the experience of the disciple, in looking for the Guru, he may find true Wisdom. Studying with the Guru will help, but the discipleship is the means of developing Atmic Wisdom.

"The King without true wisdom tried many means of attaining self wisdom, but he was working under illusion, as he thought that he would gain by giving gifts, bathing in Holy Water and observing of religious laws. These did not set him free from his mental suffering. At last he turned to his Queen and said: 'I am giving up everything in this world, but, I have one desire,—to go to the forest and live there a peaceful life, as delusion of wealth or pain do not hunt there. The bliss that is the highest attainable is in the forest; so let me go.'

"The Queen said: 'Everything will be ready and ripe at the time, I pray you do not go?'

"The King said: 'Do not interfere with my plans. You are young, and shall rule in my place, as it is the wife's duty not to languish at the absence of her husband, but to protect those who are near her.'

"The King gave an order that the city should be patrolled that night, that everyone should remain at home, within the house. That night the King made his way to the forest. After walking for two weeks he reached a spot in the Mandara Hills, which are surrounded by beautiful pools and wild flowers. He made a hut of leaves, a cloth bag for fruit, and a place for meditation. Then he started his practice; the first hour, for religious rites, the second and third, gathering flowers for God's worship, fourth, eating fruits; at night, chanting Mantras, thus the King did his tapas.

"Next morning the Queen found the King had gone to the woods, leaving behind his Kingdom, wealth and Queen. She pitied the poor King, and wanted to know where he had gone, so she levitated and roamed in the sky. She appeared to Sidhas (psychic persons), as beautiful as the shining moon. She saw her husband in the forest, meditated upon what she should do, and reached the conclusion she would not disturb him. She thought it would be better to let him master himself; so she returned to her palace without letting him see her.

"The Queen issued a proclamation to her people, stating that her husband was away on a secret mission. For eight years she ruled with royal grace of equal justice to all, while the poor King suffered a life of privation and penance in the forest.

"Realizing that the time had come for her to again see her husband, she went forth one night through the air. She alighted on a nearby hill, where she saw a decrepit and care worn, old man, whom at first she did not recognize as her husband. But her clear vision soon discovered that it was indeed he, and she cried out with her grief, to see, through dire ignorance, the King bent, groaning in pain. The Queen thought, I have power to confer Atmic Wisdom on him at this moment, but he will reject me as his young wife, so I shall not appear before him in this form. I shall change to another form to accomplish my purpose. As his mind is now ripe for Atmic Wisdom, a single word from me will show him the way to that blessed state, at this time. At this hour a rare opportunity was at hand. She changed her form from woman to man by the power of Samayan (the highest power of the Raja Yogin), and descended from the sky before the King. The King saw the form of a young Brahman standing in the air before him.

"The King paid due respect to him, and asked him to be seated. The young Brahman returned due respect to the King of true Tapas.

"The King said: 'By your gracious visit I am greatly benefited, as you are my Guru.'

"The young Brahman replied: 'Who in this world has such great qualities as you possess? May you live long. May your mind be filled with Divine Peace and be free from all delusions of the world. You are performing very high Tapas, as you have given up everything for the sake of liberation. You are performing Tapas as trying, as meeting the point of the sword.'

"The King said: 'You being a God, are well aware of my condition. May I ask your name, and who you are?'

"The young Brahman replied: 'I am the son of Rishi Narada,

whose Atmic Wisdom shines like the sun. At my birth I was taken into the presence of Brahma, who paved my way to Atmic Wisdom. As I was His grandson, He named me Kumbha Muni. My mother is Saraswati (Mother of Wisdom). I continually study the Vedas.'

"The King believed every word of the Kumbha Muni. The Muni asked the King: 'What is your name and what is your origin?'

"The King answered: 'From the pains of this world I came here for peace. My name is Sikhithwaya. I have given up my kingship as my mind was always binding me to the cycle of rebirth. I try my best to free myself from pains, but they are increasing. O Muni, the milk has surely turned to poison.'

"Kumbha Muni then replied: 'O King, without a Guru, the bliss of Atmic Wisdom is not to be obtained; tapas and mantras are merely a waste of time, O King. He who has not the Atmic Wisdom, but follows his duty of action is the best. Unselfish action will remove the impure desires; doing good karma will bring about heavenly bliss, and pure desire does not make any fresh karma, but the impure one does. If you know that all is Brahma, then ignorance is destroyed; the impure desires will never arise. If the impure desires are controlled, then old age and death are also controlled, and brings one to the highest state of Brahma.

"'The mind associated with impure desires is ignorance itself, but free from impure desires it is Wisdom itself. If through Wisdom, the Soul realizes Reality, then one is free from the chain of rebirth.

"'When all the wise, even Brahma, have said the attainment of Wisdom is the highest bliss, why do you not try to attain it? Why do you not try to find whence came this Universe? Why are you killing time here in ignorance? Why not try to find a Guru and from him learn what is bondage and what, liberation? Go to those who have clear vision over all. They are the embodiment of wisdom. Engage ceaselessly in enquiring, then indeed you will find the real, the reality, which is the means of emancipation.'

"The King cried with joy: 'O Guru, I have learned all this attainment of the way to bliss, and pure wisdom, by your grace. I have left the company of the wise through ignorance, came to this forest to suffer, but now I am freed from pain, by your kindness. I believe it is your duty, as you are within the forest, to point the way to bliss. you are my friend, you are my Guru, you are my parent. I shall be steadfast as your disciple. Please accept me as your disciple. Lead me in the path you have realized; you are equal to Brahma. Teach me the Oneness that sets people free from all pain, and into the consciousness of blissful truth.'

"Kumbha Muni said: 'I can teach you if you will concentrate your mind, which has been roaming, from place to place. Without concentration, my words will not be of any help to you.'

"The King promised to believe and concentrate on the words of the Muni. The Muni said: 'First you should have full confidence in my words, as a child has in the words of his father. O King, hear what you will not understand; I will relate again the hidden meaning. In the olden days there was a man of wealth and great knowledge, but alas, he was without Atmic Wisdom. This man went in search of Chintamuni, a wish-fulfilling jewel. In the days when he was searching to find the lucky stone, which was bright and shining as the moon, the man without understanding passed by the lucky stone. He thought it might be only a common stone, as he could not find the lucky stone in such a short space of time. He thought, I am not pure, and I am only a poor man. So he left the lucky stone beside the road, and went on hunting. After a long search, weary and worn by hardships, a Sidha—a man of psychic powers—saw the poor man looking for the lucky stone. So he thought he would fool the poor, deluded man who had passed by without recognizing the lucky stone. The Sidha threw a piece of glass in front of the man, which, as soon as he saw it, he picked up, thinking surely it must be the lucky stone. He had passed by the real lucky stone and picked up instead the simple ball of glass. He was overjoyed and gave away all his wealth, with the hope that his lucky stone would bring him anything he desired. So he went to the forest, with the hope that he would find happiness there, as the lucky stone was supposed to bring him anything for which he wished. In the forest he tried to have the lucky stone bring forth the thing he wanted, but it did not bring forth anything, for the reason it was not a lucky stone at all, it was merely a ball of glass. The poor, deluded man brought all the hardships upon himself, suffering alone and without wealth.

"I will tell another story about an elephant, that will help you in the understanding of pure Wisdom.

"In the midst of a forest there lived an elephant, the most gigantic of its kind. A Mahout of the forest followed the elephant and trapped him. His tusks were very long, sharp and dangerous. The Mahout fettered him with chains, and started to bring him to the city, tied to another elephant. This gigantic elephant became mad with pain caused by the chains, as well as the loss of his liberty. With the help of his powerful tusks he shook himself free. The Mahout seated on this elephant became frightened, and fell to the ground. The giant elephant, bewildered by his freedom, passed over the Mahout without hurting him, and raced to the security of the forest. The Mahou, getting to his feet and alarmed at the loss of his beast of wealth, went after the elephant and found him in the depth of the forest. The Mahout selected a spot where he knew the elephant would pass. Then he dug a trench and covered it with leaves. The elephant after a long time came to the place and fell into the trench. This time the Mahout fastened the elephant more securely. So again, the powerful animal was enslaved.

"'Had this gigantic elephant stepped on the Mahout, whom once he shook from his back and laid prostrate upon the ground, he might easily have crushed him or dashed out his brains, then he would not have been captured again and deprived of his precious liberty. Likewise, he who does not think of the result of evil living, and that it would surely bring him to grief.'

"The King asked the Muni: 'Please give the reason why you narrated the story of this Lucky Stone, and the story of the elephant?'

"Kumbha Muni replied: 'The man who had all wealth and knowledge, without pure Wisdom, went in search of the Lucky Stone. That man is like yourself, for, although you are well

46

versed in knowledge, you have not attained poise and peace of mind. This lesson, I meant to convey, by telling the story of the Lucky Stone. In order to overcome suffering and hypocrisy and attain true renunciation, you have forsaken your kingdom, wealth, wife and relations, which were the real Lucky Stone, and you came to the forest, which is the stone of glass.

"'The true renunciation was developing in you, little by little, in the midst of your worldly surroundings, but your mind was led astray by the wrong ideal of renunciation. By delusion your mind was enveloped as by a dark cloud, instead of being illumined, by the clear light of Spiritual understanding. This renunciation of yours is not the renunciation which generates true happiness. With the hopes that you might attain illumination, or the realization of TRUTH—that which is real—you gave up everything that men hold dear. You have lost the Lucky Stone and are holding to the false, the stone of glass.

"'The wise say that those who reject the enjoyment which comes from their daily lives, and the mind which is filled with imaginary things, are self-destructive. By giving up your all, and running to the forest your mind did not attain Divine peace, even when the valuable Lucky Stone was laid before you. Then what advantage is to be gained by finding the stone of glass?

"'The gigantic elephant, I also applied to you. The two long tusks are discrimination and indifference. Your ignorance is the driver which inflicted suffering upon you, as the elephant was caused to suffer by the driver (the Mahout). The chain and fetters stand for desires. The chain and fetters which bound the elephant will wear out, but the bonds of desire become stronger every day. As the elephant shook itself free from the chains, so you gave up your kingdom. Throwing the Mahout, or driver of the elephant,—stands for overcoming ignorance by the power of indifference to objects, or the fruits of your work. If we overcome impure desires, then ignorance and rebirth will be destroyed.

"'To abandon the delusion of wealth, by sheer asceticism, will never dispel the ghost, but if the delusion of wealth is destroyed through discrimination, then the ghost of ignorance will leave forever.

"'At the time you reached this forest your ignorance was laid on the ground before you, but you did not cut its head off with the true renunciation. The great elephant did not kill the Mahout, who was once laid on the ground at his feet. At that time if the elephant had put one foot upon the Mahout, then he would not have been made to fall into the trench, and suffer when he was imprisoned there.

"'But, O King, you have suffered more than the elephant here in the forest. You threw away the Lucky Stone, that was true renunciation, but why did you not follow the advice of your wife? But you came to this forest and picked up the stone of glass, which was not worth anything.'

"The King declared: 'I have given up my kingdom, my dear wife and all. Is this not true renunciation, O Teacher?'

"The Muni replied: 'True, you have given up your kingdom,

your wife and all, but that is not renunciation, as you are a slave to your desires, even now. But by giving up all of them, you will attain the blessed state of Brahma.'

"The King said: 'All right, I will give up this forest and hills, I have no desire for them; now, I have made the true renunciation.'

"The Muni again said: 'Giving up this beautiful forest, will not make the true renunciation, as long as you have with you impure desires. When you give them up, then only, will you attain divine joy.'

"The King answered: 'If this is not true renunciation, then, I will give up the rest.'

"So the King threw his garments and all that he had into the fire and presented himself to the Muni and said: 'Now, by your grace, I have freed myself of all things and thoughts that were only bondage, and the seed of the rebirth. By giving up all desires I have set myself free, and attained true renunciation by your kindness. What else remains to be done, O Teacher?'

"The Muni replied: 'You have not done anything. What you call a true renunciation is only vain delusion.'

"The King said: 'While I remain within this body, the five snakes, which are the sense organs remain. Therefore, I shall give them up in your presence.'

"So the King prepared to kill himself.

"The Muni stopped him by saying: 'What foolish thing are you trying to do? Is your body holding you from progress? What will you gain by giving up your body? To kill or destroy your body is not true renunciation. O King, if you will give up the seed or cause of this body, which is the seed of rebirth, then you will make the true renunciation.'

"The King besought the Muni to tell him how he might give up or control the cause, or the seed of the body.

"The Muni said: 'The Wise say the mind, with its thoughts, called by many names, is one. The cause is attached to delusive objects. This restless mind forms the Universe and bondage. It is the mind which is the seed of all karma, and moves this body to and fro, like a tree in the wind. Controlling this mind is true renunciation and Godly Bliss. O King, all other renunciations are not true.

"'After reaching the true renunciation you will be illumined in mind, free from oscillation; then you will recognize your true self with the self of Brahma, and you will be radiant with glory.'

"The King asked: 'What is the cause of the mind? What is its true nature? How should I master it? O Guru, enlighten me.'

"The Muni answered: 'The true nature of the mind is determined by the desires, as mind and desires are one. Know, O King, the ideal of the "I" (ego), which is the house in which exists all qualities of good and evil: this, is the seed of the mind. The first sprout that comes out of this seed is Egoism and originates without form. It's a perception is by inner experience. This sprout is called Buddhi (intellect). From this little shoot the many branches known as thoughts take their origin through differentiation. The thought of the mind, the reason and intelligence, called by different names are really only Egoism. If you try to cut off the branches (desires) of the tree of the mind, you will not succeed, as the branches will produce more and more, through desires. But if you cut the root of the tree with the ax of Wisdom, then the branches will die themselves, and the karma that causes the branches will disappear with them. But to merely cut off the branches, will not harm the tree of the mind. You should cut the root of the tree or through virtuous actions overcome the ideal of the Ego.'

"The King said: 'I am the Nature, that pure absolute conscious-ness which evolves. preserves, and destroys everything. I do not know the cause of the "I", which is the nature of Wisdom. I have not been able to find the means which will remove the Egoism, the seed of the treacherous mind. My mind betrayed me as I tried to overthrow this Ego, but it clings to me.'

"The Muni said: 'No effect can be found without a cause. So search within to find the cause of the Egoism that is always within you. Answer me, O King.'

"The King answered: 'The cause of this impure Egoism is the knowledge of the mind. How have I become mixed with this knowledge? I sink back when the knowledge of objects arises. How am I to arise above the objective world?'

"The Muni answered: 'If you tell me the cause of knowledge, then I will give you the means to arise above it.'

"The King then said: 'The existence of the illusory objects of knowledge is produced through mind. If the illusory objects cease to exist, then no knowledge arises. Then the seed of the mind, Egoism will be absorbed.'

"The Muni answered: 'As the illusory objects exist so the knowledge, but the illusory objects are unreal. Then what is the basis for knowledge, O King?'

"The King replied: 'Tell me first, O Guru, how can the body which enjoys all karma be unreal?'

"The Muni answered: 'This body, arising through karma, cannot be the cause, therefore, neither the effect of intelligence, as it is itself illusory or nonexistent. The Egoism and all other illusory objects which arise through the delusion of knowledge are not real. Therefore, all the objects which are not of the nature of cause and effect, are not real, any more than the mistaken conception of the snake in the rope.'

"The King said: 'All are the creation of Brahma, who was alone in the beginning of the Universe. How, then, can you say that Brahma is not the cause of it?'

"The Master answered: 'Prior to the creation, the Parabrahma (Supreme Spirit) alone shone as Truth, which is nondual and quiescent. He alone is without a second, then how can Brahma be the cause?'

"The King asked: 'Is not Parabrahma the cause?'

"The Master replied: 'Parabrahma is the emancipation, the imperishable, birthless, deathless, without beginning and without end. The non-dual and unspeakable can not be reached by thought. How can Parabrahma be the cause which is above the reach of the mind and thought? How can one be an actor and an audience? As it would be impossible, it must follow that this Universe is not created by any one, nor is self-created. The Supreme Will of the Absolute Consciousness is Brahma, nothing else is the one true Wisdom. All the objects created out of that Wisdom can be said to be none other than the form of that Wisdom.

"'All is Brahma itself. Realize the one Reality, which will destroy ignorance, never to rise again. There is no other path through which to destroy the delusion of karma, which will surely vanish when ignorance and illusion are destroyed. The Brahmic state will be attained, then the mind through all-pervading Wisdom will merge into Paramatma (Universal soul, Supreme Self), and will never be evolved into new creations by thoughts. That which is called Brahma, through the Atmic Tattva (highest pure wisdom of the self), is none other than the latent aspect of the Universe.'

"The King replied: 'All that you have taught me is very reasonable. As before creation there was no Creator; so there is really no Universe, there are no objects; illusory things do not really exist according to your clear teaching. I understand the reality of myself and recognize that external objects do not really exist. I have worshipped myself through many substances. Now I realize that all were unreal, through this wise teaching. I have become one without a thought of a second, as one Akasa (ether) is everywhere.'

"Through the Muni's reasoning, the King realized his reality, also, the true discrimination of time and space.

"Mental activity is to understand the Universe, in all its different aspects. They have existed in your mind a long time, but they will depart, leaving only Brahma alone.

"The King was illumined by the Wisdom he attained and was immediately freed from Maya. He reached the state of Brahma or Brahmic state and sank into Samadhi.

"After some hours he awakened from meditation, and the Master asked: 'Are you free from all passion? Have you enjoyed the Brahmic Bliss? Have you enjoyed the Brahmic seat which is fullness of all wealth? Have you attained Atmic Wisdom? Are you freed from all delusion? Have you met that which is worth meeting? Have you seen the Blessed One that is worthy to be seen?'

"The King replied: 'I have now the eternal peace. I have indeed reached the Brahmic state, which is above all. With your kind help I have reached the Brahmajnan state, the powerful state of Divine Wisdom. O Guru, why was I not able to reach this high state before?'

"The Muni answered: 'When mind becomes absolutely at rest and one sees all with impartial eyes, with vision turned inward, with all impurities of the mind gone, then it is easy for the Master to help the disciple, as there is no doubt in the mind of the student.

"'Doubt is the big stone in the road of divine wisdom. The king attained the wealth of wealth, bliss of bliss, which is the divine wisdom, and the highest good.'

"'O Guru,' said the King, 'Are not the Jivanmukta performing actions through their mind?'

"The Muni answered: 'The mind is nothing without desire; mind and desires bind one to rebirth. If one knows the divine self, there is no fear of rebirth. Truth sets them free. Those Jivanmukta have realized the reality; therefore, their Minds do not generate impure desires, but generate pure desires. With pure desire you do not create rebirth. The lower mind or work done under the influence of the lower mind produces cause; but the higher mind or work done under the influence of the higher mind does not produce any cause.'

"So the King gave up the idea of doing good for reward, but sought to do good for the sake of good. Give up the idea of going to heaven, then you will shine like the Light of Lights that is in all and is everywhere,—which really you are. Let the lower mind go, that has a hankering to go from place to place, from earth to sky, and from sky to earth.

"With the control of the lower mind, the rebirth is also controlled,—becomes peaceful, immovable, then you become one with pure Wisdom (motion and non-motion).'

"'O Guru', said the King. 'How am I to attain that state where motion and non-motion is one?'

"The Muni replied: 'As the ocean is rippled by the waves, but is still one, so all the Universe is non-dual, is Absolute Consciousness, compelling, drawing intelligence unto itself. The ignorant will not understand the difference, how the Truth and Brahma is the Universe itself,—motion in itself,—this Universe Created by itself. If you realize this outwardly, then the blessed state is yours. This merely reverses the appearance, seen as the real cause, as the rope in the dark appears as a snake.

"'By following pure wisdom, and association with the wise., then the spiritual vision will develop; then only can you truly realize as I have explained to you—this creation and the destruction of the Universe.

"'If you practise according to your will, do your duty conscientiously, then you will not fail to attain the Brahmic state. Does not that do away with all the differences that arise from delusion and ignorance?'

"The Muni disappeared, and the King thought to himself: 'How can I understand that I am All Peace, All Rest, All Bliss, and Absolute Truth?' The King sank into Samadhi, which is above all pain, misery and the Universe. It is True Peace, and True Silence. The Mui resumed the tender form of the Queen, and went through the sky by levitation to her chamber in the palace. There she again graciously ruled over her people for three years.

"With her higher mind and power she changed her feminine body for a masculine form, and again visited the King, as she was teaching her King in the form of a Muni.

"When she reached the forest where the King was, she found him in a seedless Samadhi. To acquaint him with her arrival she caused the forest to re-echo with her voice. This did not disturb the King, as he was not awakened from the seedless Samadhi. Though she shook him vigorously, he evinced no evidence of her presence.

"'This is truly wonderous', said the Queen, 'he has merged into the seat of Brahma, I will concentrate on his finer body. If I find any residue of truth typifying the seed of intelligence in his heart, I will join my King and live with him joyfully; otherwise, I shall have to give up my feminine form, and myself obtain the Brahmic State, then I will be free from rebirth.'

"The Queen concentrated on the finer form of the King, and found there was still a residue of good qualities in the heart of the King."

Ram asked: "When one's mind has control, and has merged into the inner vision, how can there still be a residue of good or bad qualities in the heart?"

Rishi Vashisht answered: "Like the tree, the branches, flowers, and fruit are all contained in the seed, so the cause of intelligence, like Satwa, always rests in the heart. The Jivanmukta who has controlled his mind, does not die and is not affected by diseases or pains,—he is living in the world, but above the world, like the Lotus flower that lives in the water, but does not get wet. Even in the heart of the Jivanmukta, the cause of the intelligence, latent in the heart, is like the tree that is in the seed.

"O Ram, the Great Yogi Queen gave up the grosser body of the Muni and merged into the finer form of the King, that is higher consciousness,—without beginning or end. She caused it to vibrate and return to her body, as a bird to its cage. Again in the Muni form, she chanted the Divine Song, which brought the King to consciousness, as the rays of the Sun made the Lotus flower bloom.

"The King saw his dear Guru sitting before him. With great joy he praised the Muni (Queen).

"The Muni said: 'From the day I parted from you my mind did not find blessed peace. Even in the Higher Heavens, there is no joy for me, except with you.'

"The King replied: 'I have obtained this blessed state by your favor, and am freed from all pain and misery. Even the Higher Heavens did not give me the blessed joy that I have from the seedless Samadhi. Now I am Master of ail. Blessed Peace is mine. I can roam freely in Heaven and on earth.'

"The Muni asked: 'Have you tasted the Brahmic Bliss, God—like joy, which is above all pleasure and pains? Have you given up all older thoughts from which arise the ideas of, this is mine, and that is thine? Can you hold an equal vision over all? Are you able to do your daily duty without effort, or being affected by it? Are you free from hate and love? Have you realized it all?'

"The King replied: 'Indeed, I have acquired all the spiritual benefits. I have known all that is worth knowing, have seen all that is worth seeing, there is nothing that I long to see or hear.'

"So the Muni and the King with great respect for one another, enjoyed great bliss and Divine joy, as one in mind and one in everything. They had destroyed delusion of the Maya, by pure Wisdom. They were firm like the Himalayan Mountains, not to be shaken by the rustling winds.

"The Queen in the form of the Master, found by the power of Samyam (highest concentration of the Raja Yogi), that the King's mind was pure and free from all illusion. She also thought, if one is filled with wisdom, shouldn't he enjoy the joy that comes without seeking; or how can it be said he or she had true wisdom? She thought she would interrogate the King further. 'There is a festival in the Higher Heavens today,' said the Queen, 'I shall be there, I will return tonight.'

"The Queen discarded her heavy male body, and resumed her own beautiful form. She reached her palace by air, and performed her Queenly duties all day. After sunset she again went forth by levitating her body to the forest where the King was. The Queen resumed her disguise of the Muni's form, descended before her husband with dejected mien, long and downcast heart.

"The King rising said: 'My Perfect One, my Guru, what has affected you,—you are suffering from pain? What is it? May you overcome it as a person of Wisdom. You are not affected by pain or joy, as the water falling on the duck's back does not affect her.'

"The Muni related the following story: 'The true Jnani who visions all with an equal eye, and sees all in all, will never be a true Jnani as long as he does not use his organs, as long as he possesses a body. Otherwise, that person is an imposter. The ignorant are those who do not perform their karma but try to avoid them. They will suffer as they are trying to separate the oil from the mustard seed, which is inseparable. As long as the body exists, pains and pleasures remain. They who try to do away with affections and so forth, are like a man who tries to cut air with a sword. Pain and an impure body always go together. The Brahma has the organs of Karmaendriya (organs of action), and the Jnanendriya (organs of sense), and follows the path which is forever followed by the ignorant and wise, which has moved the concourse with Universal Law.

"'The Wise ones daily do their duty, as long as they stay in their bodies. They are not affected by performing actions, but the ignorant mind is never at peace, is ever moving and affected by pain and pleasure.

"'The Cause of my pain—it is not pain when told to those we love. This morning I went to the Higher Heavens for the meeting. I went there by air. After the meeting, when coming through the sky to this place, I saw before me the Rishi Divwasa coming through the clouds. I said to him, you are ill clad; and I acted like a silly woman whereupon the Rishi cursed me. He said: "You are acting like a woman, so your form will change to female from now on, every night." Hearing this I begged for pardon, but the Rishi disappeared. This is the cause of my distress. I have to change to a woman's form every night. I am ashamed.'

"'Do not grieve,' said the King, 'changing your form will not change you from wise to ignorant, only the unwise can be so affected by pain.'

"'The sun is setting,' the Muni said to the King, 'and the change in me is taking place.'

"The King said: 'You are wise, and you know the true path, so you shall not be affected by the change.' So they retired for the night.

"At dawn the Queen was again the Muni. So she was a man by day, and by night a woman.

"'O King, how long, I ask, are we going to live like this? I want to have a husband, but I cannot find one to equal you in the three worlds. You should marry me, without the fear of Heaven or Hell.'

"The King was prepared for her proposal, and made ready for the marriage rites. White silken robes were procured by the power of thought. When the sun set, the marriage ceremony took place. Every other day the King went into Samadhi, then the Queen would go to her Palace, perform her Queenly duties, and return to the forest before the King awakened from his Samadhi. Thus the time passed away.

"The Queen wanted to enquire into her husband's mind, so one day with power of her Yoga, she created a heaven of illusion in the forest, also an illusory God to appear before the King. When the King saw God and His Heaven, he asked: 'What good karma have I performed to induce you to visit me?' 'I am attracted by your love and purity, and I came to take you to the Higher Heavens. It is fitting for you to leave. The Divine Maidens will wait upon you, and will always be at your command. O King, you will live there as long as you wish. This place is not good enough for you to live in; Heaven is the place for you, and you will not want to leave it. For that reason I came to take you.'

"The King with a gesture of gentle remonstrance, replied: 'I have known all the pleasure of Heaven. One locality is the same as another to me. Wherever I am, there is my Heaven and Bliss. Be pleased to return to your throne. I have no desire to go with you.' Hearing this, the illusory God disappeared. The Queen felt that the King had attained Master control.

"The Queen decided to try the King further. It chanced that the King was sitting at the Holy Ganges watching the Moon rise. The Queen, with power of thought, created a lover and embraced him. When the King came out of his trance and found his wife in the company of another man, he returned to the river at once, without disturbing his peace of mind. When the Queen went to the King, with embarrassment, she appeared before her husband, ashamed. Without evincing the least sign of anger, he said tenderly: 'Why did you, my dear, leave your lover so soon? If you wish you may go back to him and gratify your passion.' Thus spoke the king without anger.

"'It is the duty,' said the Queen, 'of a good husband to overlook the faults of his wife, who is ignorant and carried away by her emotions; and I am trusting that you will forgive me.'

"The King replied: 'The sun may rise in the West, but never will anger arise in me. A house may be built in the air, but anger will never arise in me. I have controlled both love and hate.'

"The Queen understood that her husband was really a Muni, and had attained the pure Wisdom of Divine Peace.

"'The time has now arrived for me to show myself in my true colors, and let him see me as I really am.' She assumed her Queenly body and appeared before him. The King beheld his Queen, whom he had left at his Kingdom twenty years ago. He could not believe his eyes.

"'Am I beholding my Queen? Who are you, please speak?'

"The Queen replied: 'Yes, I am your wife, with whom you have lived for nearly one hundred years. You left me at the Palace when you retired to the forest.'

"'So dearest, it was you who came in the guise of Master Kunbhamuni to save me?'

"'It was I who took the form of the Muni; it was I who gave you Divine Wisdom; it was I who tested your Wisdom. Now go into Samadhi; then you will understand all that has been happening,' said the Queen.

"The King went into Samadhi, the Brahmic or Universal consciousness. In that state he saw all the events and remembered them from the time he vacated his kingdom, to the time of his appearing to his Queen Chundalai in her feminine body. When he came out of his Samadhi, he was blessed with divine peace and joy. With joy he looked upon his wife who was standing before him. He embraced her, who was the embodiment of pure love and grace.

"The King could not find words with which to thank his wife. Later he began to speak: 'Through your great Wisdom you have saved me, who was crying in the darkness from ignorance. Who is there in the Universe to equal you? You are the Blessed Light, dispelling the fear of the ignorant. How can I repay you for all that you have done for me? You are on equality with the Divine Mother.'

"'I saw you in despair,' lovingly replied the Queen. 'Your self-imposed penances were destroying your body. That kind of penance is used only by the ignorant. I came to save and lift you from worldly pain. Do not praise me. I did my duty. Tell me, dear husband, are you free from the world's troubles? Have you reached the divine state which will not be affected by action or thought?'

"'All doubt and desire have vanished from my mind,' said the King. 'I shall never fall through the senses. I have become like Akasa. I am above pain or pleasure. I have attained the highest Samadhi. There is no joy like the joy of Samadhi. I have reached the highest state; I am the Sun of the Suns; I am the Light of the Lights; I am pure Wisdom; I am the Absolute Consciousness. I realize my Reality, which is none other than THAT (God). My wife, you are my Spiritual Teacher. I worship you.'

"'What do you intend to do next?' questioned the Queen.

"'From now on,' answered the King, 'according to your dictates, I shall perform my duties. I will live in the world, but not of it, like the Lotus flowers which grow in the lake but never get wet.'

"'If you are willing to do as I say, then let us go back and reign over our Kingdom, as Jivanmuktas.'

"'I will do as you say,' replied her husband.

"The Queen then created an elephant. It was decorated with rubies and other gems. They both mounted the elephant's back, and when they came near the town, with the power of her mind she created an army to escort them into the city. They were received by their people.

"The King and Queen were enthroned, and ruled wisely and well for ten thousand years, and then they gave up the bodies and attained emancipation of the Soul.

"O Ram, do your daily karma and pure wisdom will develop in you. You will reach the Blessed state Which the King and Queen have attained, Liberation." Thus spoke the great Rishi Vashisht of Wisdom, to Ram.

Six

THE GREAT EGOIST—BALI

Rishi Vashisht continued: "The illumination of wisdom came like the dawn to the heart of Pavana, who had been initiated by his brother, the Muni Punya. Both of these brothers, having attained Atmic wisdom, lived in the forest. For many years they enjoyed the quiet pleasures of solitude and at last reached the calm of bodiless bliss—like lights which have consumed both wick and oil. For this is the fate of all beings.

"If one, in his many incarnations is related to all, where then, is the necessity of love or hate? The most reasonable course is to forego extreme and excessive desires, not to enlarge upon them. If desire is allowed to flourish lit becomes food for contemplation. When desire passes, so does the structure of thought built about it, collapse and perish. This is indeed the truth.

"O Ram, mount the great edifice of renunciation and behold in spiritual vision this insignificant universe palpitating with unruly desires—then you will indeed know that you lack nothing. This exalted state contains the truth of Brahma without. impurity, delusion or the plague of ignorance. If this state be attained by faith even though the intelligence is meager, its devotees will not be subject to delusion. Therefore, O Ram, lead thus your life.

"With the progressive development of intelligence and the exercise of a fine discrimination all pain will cease. Even though one may find a close ally in a Guru, it is only through individual energy and will, that all pains arising from association with kinsmen and heterogeneity can be destroyed. Having labored diligently through Atmic enquiry, books of wisdom, and noble benevolence, your mind is forced to follow the Atmic life—then pain will cease. The collective wealth of all worlds will not compare with the happiness arising from the blissful mind which has found emancipation.

"Like a sandal protects the foot, however stony the path, so also, does the mind fill the whole of creation with purest joy. A mind filled to the fullest with neutrality of vision will never entertain mundane desire; nor a mind confused by conflicting desires ever have its grievances completely redressed. A mind free from desire yields pure thoughts, as readily as Muni Agastya sipped the waters of the ocean in the space of a moment; the radiance of the full moon has not such refulgence, nor does Lakshmi (Goddess of Fortune) reposing on fragrant Lotus grant such a boon.

"The ghosts of desire will dim the lustre of the stainless mind just as clouds hide the moon, or black stains deface polished stone. Liberation means only the destruction of the impurities of the mind and this mind is developed only when desire and fears of rebirth are destroyed. If this is not possible, O Ram, you shall arrive at wisdom by the path followed by the great Bali. Such a course is beneficial."

Thereupon Ram asked him to relate the story of Bali.

Rishi Vashisht replied: "There once lived a great king who was also a great egoist. He reigned over Patala as an emperor. The whole world trembled beneath his autocratic rule; even the gods were overpowered and humbled before him. He was the son of the noble Virochana, and reigned mightily for ten million years.

"One day he mounted to the parapet atop his palace—his palace which was studded with gems brought from the Mahameru Mountains. There in solitude he spoke the travail of his mind. He was satiated with the material pleasure of his world and his speech was replete with bitterness.

"'Of what avail is this undisputed sovereignty which has enabled me to enjoy the wealth of these three worlds, when I reflect that the pleasures of wealth are but fleeting, and that I repeat today's actions again tomorrow with only a gain of momentary happiness? Enjoyed incidents do recur again; ornaments worn proudly yesterday are put on again to-day. We observe that even the intelligent do not become appeased by these recurrences and are not ashamed to enjoy them again, like children who feast repeatedly on sweets.

"'Thy cycle of days, months, years and yugas roll on, and the old is ever old, though decked in the changing garments of the mode.

"'Has the faithful performance of my duties improved my life in the slightest degree? What will bring me possession of THAT and free me of action and its results? Where is the path which will lead me to THAT which is peace, free from illusion?'

"Deep in reflection he sought the Principle which is eternal and at last was rewarded by the solution. With eyes flashing with joy he said: 'It was in this very place that I enquired about this Principle from my omniscient father, Virochana. He explained then the manner in which I might remove my doubts when I asked him, what is that incomparable state in which the illusions of pain and pleasure are lost, wherein the mind's delusions find oblivion, and where desires are uprooted?' I begged that he would describe to me the attainment of that goal which knows not the 'restraint of desires and the gloomy despondency of the mind.

"'Tell me, O Father, I beseech you what is the state which is wholly permeated with Absolute bliss? O you, Knower of the Supreme, enlighten me and release me from the torment of doubts which arise!'

"And thus Virochana replied: 'Listen to my words. There is a beautiful country which is illimitable and all pervading. In it the worlds arise and into it the worlds are absorbed. In this country there are not the five grand elements, nor are there hills, forest, temples, Devas or even the ancient souls. Illumination is the name of the King who exists there, alone. He is omnipotent, omniscient, the cause of all, perfectly quiescent and refulgent. He is Silence itself. He will unfailingly cause all acts to be performed by a minister appointed by him. The instant that a thought arises in the minister, the idea, though previously nonexistent, immediately crystallizes into actuality and mysteriously disappears. The minister enjoys nothing by his own right nor does he know anything. Acting always in concert with the King he is able to do all things. Though the minister stands always in the presence of the King, the King remains invisible and solitary.'

"So said the father to his son. The son had listened appreciatively to the words of his father. Now he questioned: 'What is the character of this enlightened country which is without disease and misery, which though apart, yet pervades all? How can it be reached? By what means can it be attained? Who is the immortal King of that strange country? Who is his minister? Who is the mighty King, who, as if in sport, will make me ruler of this universe?'

"His father answered: 'Who is able to overstep the rigorous law of the powerful minister? Even though the hosts of the world beleaguer him, they can never overpower him. Though spears be hurled against him they will be as futile as flowers flung at a stone wall. Only the King can command obeisance from his minister, for it was easier to move the great Himalayas than to bring Him into subjection. It takes a very superior intelligence to subdue the minister, for he is like an angry serpent who when trod upon will hiss and strike.

"All this, my son, is symbolic. The country in my story is liberation, incomparable and eternal; the King is Atmic Reality, inseparable from liberation and refulgent with eternal light; the minister of the King typifies the mind or intelligence. The symbol and realization of supreme authority is the subjection, control and eradication of sensual pleasures and the building-up of an indifference to them. When the mind has overcome desire, then it resembles a mischievous elephant safely caged.

"'Those unacquainted with the true books of wisdom maintain that of the four parts into which they divide time, one-half should be devoted to a study of sensual objects, one-quarter to study of the Books of Wisdom, and the remaining quarter to the worship of a blessed Guru; that if this be done, wisdom will replace ignorance.

"'The partially knowing assert that of the four divisions one should devote half the time to contemplation and worship of a Guru, a quarter to meditation upon the spiritual truths contained in the Books of Wisdom, and the remaining quarter to the study of the actions of the sensual organs. The wisdom will prevail in him, and he will know the supreme truth.

"'The third class, who are of the wise elect, affirm that liberation will be attained by those, who, dividing the concentration of the mind into four parts devote them to the four purposes of a study of the Books of Wisdom, which outline the pursuit of the path of Atmic Reality. Self-knowledge, desirelessness, worship, and worship of a Guru. May you, my son, through diligent enquiry and intelligent effort, understand Atmic worship and the subjugation of desire simultaneously. By a determined master of your desires, Atmic enquiry naturally follows, and in turn Atmic enquiry induces a relinquishment of desire. They are mutually dependent one upon the other, like the clouds which fill the ocean.

"'Having earned wealth for relieving one's kindred and dependents, one should, by the help of that wealth, promote the qualities of truthful conduct and gradually assume indifference to the world of objects and futile pleasures. This is the state reached by thos who live in Jnana. This is the glory of peace.'

"Soliloquizing thus, he asked himself: 'Who am I and what is my real nature?' After a moment's reflection he concluded that if he invoked his Guru, who had attained Realization, and should enquire of him the truth, then ignorance would forsake him. Therefore, with closed eyes he meditated affectionately upon his Guru. Thereupon his Guru took form before him, a form constituted of the blessed air. With an enraptured heart the King saluted him and spread fragrant flowers before the resplendent Guru.

"'O Beloved Guru, deign to hear my words and bless me accordingly. What is the NOW? What is there BEYOND? What is THAT which is limited? Who am I who speaks? And YOU who hear? What is this material universe? Favor me, Divinity, with answers to quiet all my doubts.'

"The Guru pondered for a moment and then replied: 'I am on my way to Heaven where dwell the immortals. Why should I take unnecessary time or waste words? Briefly, I tell you this, all the manifestations before us here are wrought of wisdom, the unmanifested is also wisdom. I, who speak, am wisdom, and pure wisdom are you, who hear. The entire universe is naught but all-full wisdom. Take these conclusions, impress them upon your mind and meditate upon the Reality of Wisdom. If you can accept Reality, you will attain the Supreme state. The Saptarishi has just now entered a new state; therefore, I shall pass.' So saying the Guru of Bali retired.

"Contemplating the truth of his Guru's words, he became convinced that ALL IS WISDOM. This earth is none other than the manifestation of Wisdom; the three worlds are Jnana; my real nature is Jnana, the fates are Jnana. I have become the shining Brahmic One, who scintillates undimmed by the visual or the sensual. I have become the One principle, which unbound by objectives, pervades all at one and the same time—intelligence itself.

"Mentally vibrating to Om, which is the true significator of Absolute Wisdom, Bali entered a trance-like state, which was free from thought, desire or doubts, and there he remained statue-like in Samadhi for a long period.

"Thus did the Emperor Bali remain motionless, as the flame of a lighted lamp in a sheltered, windless place. And since he was illumined by the Truth, unstained by love or hate, his mind merged into Divine Peace. Such a condition can best be compared to clear, autumnal sky.

"Seeking their Emperor, his courtiers found him deep in

Samadhi.

"After a long time, Bali awoke and went about his regal duties, with his mind being free from desire and egotism. His pure mind was never again flurried in adversity or prosperity, neither did he lose himself in either pleasure or pain. Thus his equable gaze viewed all impartially, however numerous were the hosts of good and had thoughts that arose in his mind. As the procession of countless objects passed before him, he controlled them all.

"So shall you, O Ram, pillion your mind, roving amid the pleasures of this and higher worlds, in the centre of your heart. Wherever your mind stumbles like an awkward child and falls into sensuality, you must lift it to the indivisible Jnana and there let your mind become one with wisdom. By daily and consistent practice you may chain the terrible elephant of mind, so that untrammeled by pain, you will enable it to reach liberation through control."

So said the great Teacher, Rishi Vashisht.

Seven

KING JANAK

"We must understand, in the words of Muni-Kacha, that this universe in reality IS NOT, and that it is formed only by the varying intensities of the flow of consciousness. Consciousness may be compared to a powerful revolving light which leaves in darkness, that which it illumined so brightly the instant before. Therefore, when the light of consciousness reveals this universe, the universe seems real. Take away the light and the world loses reality. So it is that from conscious knowledge and Atmic wisdom the universe becomes real to us.

"To the seekers after name, fame and pleasure, the house of the mind is founded on the delusion of birth and death. But the adherents of truth will be free from these delusions, for birth is but death (or cessation of consciousness) to former life, and death is birth (or renewed consciousness) into another period of life.

"All is Brahma and the 'I' is Brahma. Relinquish the idea that the universe is something outside the 'I'. The objects of creation arising from Brahmic wisdom do not really exist, but are as the foamy spray cast up by the ocean. One principle alone Brahma is constant, enduring and eternally IS. Pleasure nor pain, nor the whirlpool of birth and death do not really exist. Brahma alone exists.

"Experience and inference teach the transient nature of fleeting pleasure and pain. Why then dwell upon them? Forget the past and the future and rest in the neutral state of truth, putting aside the duality of love and hate. Look equally upon all, steadfast in the certainty of Atmic wisdom, secure in the stronghold of mind withheld from worldly objects.

"So may you, O lotus-eyed Ram, be the crystal, which mirrors pain but does not suffer it.

"Thus Atmic wisdom will flush the dawn of the final birth. For where shall one seek the lustrous bamboo pearl, but in the bamboo clusters? For in these blessed ones, nobility, love, benevolence and clarity of intellect find residence, and these qualities of Atmic wisdom draw to them the people of the world like the melodious flute brings rapture even to the hearts of kine.

"Two paths lead to liberation. On one, the faithful following of the precepts laid down by a Guru shall let delusion fall away, to be replaced with emancipation. Peace shall come either in the immediate birth or in a succeeding birth. The other path is open to one whose mind is already bulwarked by knowledge, and who will, by meditation, cultivate the fertile seed into the full blossom of wisdom.

"Of the second path this story is related. An emperor, fearless, generous and of untold wealth once reigned over this universe. Into his domain never a taint of jealousy or envy entered. This King, Janak by name, and Videha by reputation, whose noble heart embraced the world, was a true protector of his people.

"In the first days of vernal spring King Janak walked in his charming garden among his fragrant flowers. Without its gates the guards were stationed. Strolling about, the King heard the murmuring voices of the Sidhas from the hills. Hear attentively, O Ram, the songs of the Sidhas—they who have withdrawn from the pleasures of the visible.

"Chanted a Sidha: 'In the union of the Knower and the Known lies the bliss or wisdom. Seek this wisdom, so that the unreal may become the real.'

"Another sang: 'Desire will destroy the visible. Contemplate Atmic reality—the beacon to the eagle vision of higher spirituality.'

"The chorus of voices sang: 'Having become all-pervading, he, who sits between truth and untruth, meditates always upon Atmic wisdom, the Light of Lights. To seek without God is like one who goes in quest of bright bits of glass, unmindful of the jewel blazing his own hand. Atma is attained only by those who have controlled their desires. Those who recklessly entangle themselves in the quicksands of human experience, knowing better, can only be called asses. The hissing serpents of the desirous organs must be slain by the mind; just as the great god Indra levelled the mountains to dust by his thunderbolt. The mind, free from delusion which calmly surveys all as one, will attain Atmic Reality—the plenum of complete bliss. This is liberation.'

"The sage counsels of the Sidhas, awoke consternation in the mind of King Janak. He left behind his cool scented garden, entered his palace and dismissed his attendants.

"Seeking a quiet apartment on the top floor of his palace, he gave himself to meditation upon the wise utterances of the Sidhas. In contemplation he hoped to discover the true meaning of these blissful counsellors. He thought how the people of the world were like birds forever on the wing, fluttering hither and thither from this bush to that flower, only to drop at last with weariness, and perish.

"The good King cried out in his anguish of mind: 'Annoyances beset me. Worries, doubts and circumstances enmesh me in this uncertain world. I spin about like a leaf in a whirlpool. When I reflect that time in its true nature is eternal. I cannot but deem the one hundred years of my life, as a moment in eternity. Why, then, do I value my life so greatly and allow my strong desires to throw me into confusion and dejection? What greater debasement than a mind despoiled of tranquility? That I should consider for a moment this unsettled existence. This world of pain I rule is but an atom among the countless universes. Search as I will, I can find nothing which remains constant and beneficent, even for a fleeting moment. Behold the incongruities of this world. The greatest shall be dust, even as the lowliest. Wealth! Have I fancied the riches? Name and fame! The great men of ancient times and their valorous deeds have vanished. Where, then, is the certainty that the achievements of my time shall persist?

"'The myriad worlds with their rulers and wealth have perished, like sand washed into the sea. Where, O my distraught mind, have these universes gone? So shall this, my world, go the way of eternity. My desires and my illusions have led me to believe in a permanency, which does not exist. My many deaths have taught me nothing. When shall the blessed time come when I shall seek and find THAT, which has no end? About me the objects of the world wear the shrouds of destruction. Every instant of every day, the ignorant walk the paths of perdition, their bodies enacting the baneful deeds of pleasure and pain. In youth they are unwise; maturity finds them entangled in the meshes of passion and the burden of the world bows them down in old age.

"'Harassed from birth to death, doing the deeds of desire, how can they find time to pursue virtue and seek eternal truth? Illusion dances in this world like a will-o-wisp, and my mind dances in unison with illusion—both specters of the Real in this unreal theatre.

"'Untruth is an excrescence upon the Crown of Truth, and pain thrusts its talons into the side of Virtue. Since pain is the accompaniment of pure and impure pleasure alike, how may we discern the difference between them? If between the opening and closing of my eyes many Brahmas are created and destroyed, what is my puny self before them? Great wealth breeds pain in the mind of its owner, but a thing fraught with peril, becomes a source of 'happiness, for a mind which controls it rightly. It is only the worldly life which is the source of pain. Can happiness enter a life submerged in worldliness? The tree of the ignorant mind sprouts from the root of delusion and its branches bear poisonous fruits.

"'Mind is the thinking principle. By the discipline of thought, the mind itself can easily be controlled. The extinction of delusion controls birth and death. Oh, I know at last the thief who has robbed me of the Atmic jewel of my Self. His name is Mind. Long and grievously I have suffered, I shall impale him with his own bright sword of thought.

"'Until now I have not been able to pierce the pearl of mind. Now I will string this pearl upon the strand of experience, and with it adorn my person. I have listened well to the wise counsels of the omniscient Sidhas. At last I rest in the bliss in which the great Brahma floats. The unrealities of me and you have dropped away, and I will never permit them to return. Victory is mine over the mighty adversary of mind, who despoiled me of Atmic wisdom, and pain has ceased its affliction. I have attained a life of sustained peace. Great wisdom has rolled back the ponderous door to freedom; my adoration is your.'

"Thus did King Janak rest motionless in Samadhi, having controlled the fluctuation and vacillation of his mind. After a long period of Samadhic bliss he looked anew upon his world, his vision cleared of the fog of desire. He reflected that he had no objective for which to strive in this world. His clear sight

80

scrutinized the world for illusion and found pure wisdom.

"'I know nothing,' he rejoiced, 'but my immaculate divine wisdom, the realization of my Self. I shall neither seek nor turn from any object in this world. I shall remain constant in my divine Self. Events will transpire as pre-ordained.' So saying, the King was enveloped in Brahmic bliss.

"As the warm sun in the sky, without volition or desire, causes the growth of seeds in the ground, so King Janak performed the duties, which arise daily without exaltation or longing. Giving heed neither to the past nor the future, productive as such cogitation is of discontent, King Janak met the present serenely, with an undivided heart and mind.

"The Atmic enquiry engendered by the words of the Sidhas, brought quiescence of mind, O Ram, to the ruler of the world, King Janak; for the wisdom of Atma can be attained only by the pure and beautiful Atmic enquiry, and not by following the ways of the worldly. For worldlings long for other goals than Atma, and realization comes only to those who have sought it faithfully. Therefore, O Ram, destroy ignorance, which slinks like a hungry wolf in the desert, that is the world.

"To the wise, the precious jewel of wisdom enthroned in their minds, will bring in a moment whatsoever they wish, like the Kalpa tree which produced any fruit one desired. Love and hate cannot dent the armour of those who dwell in Atmic bliss. The dense mist of egoism screening the Sun of Brahma obscures the intelligence, and will be cleared only by the heavenly wind of divine wisdom. He who aspires to the Supreme Brahmic throne must banish desires from his mind, for is not the ground well-tilled before the planting of the seed?"

Eight

SURAGHO

"Even though you pursue your appointed path through the world, O Ram, there is beneficent quietude in the throne of the All-Wise, if you but recognize the Knower with your mind. So long, Ram, as you attain the Atmic state by your constant mastery of externals, your mind will ever be inquiriing into the unlimited pure wisdom. The supreme state may be reached through Atmic enquiry; by turning aside from worldly objects, discernment of the true significance of the Books of Wisdom; one's own intelligence; initiation by a Guru; refraining from taking the life of any living thing; purity; or it can be attained by one's intelligence alone. Lacking all else, liberation will be his who is possessed of subtle and stainless intelligence and is initiated by a Guru."

Upon hearing Rishi Vashisht, Ram enquired: "The persons named by you divide into two classes. One class frees itself of pain and attains the unity of wisdom by going into Samadhi while still doing the work of the world; the other retires from action in the world and goes into Samadhi. Of these two which is superior? Please enlighten me clearly on this point."

To which Rishi Vashisht answered: "In Samadhi there is recognition of the inactivity of this world. The mind becomes completely passionless, with no concern for the world or its objects. Whether one enters Samadhi from amid the turmoil of the world, or the quiet depths of a forest, there is no difference. Both have attained complete equipoise of mind, and the incalculable fruits of the great meditation are theirs. In this state of illumination, the serenity of mind is absolute. Therefore, O Ram, it matters not by what door one enters. The sublime state of Samadhi within lies liberation.

"When the desires are extinct, the performance of actions will be as if not done, like one, who, deep in mental concentration does not hear the voices of bystanders. But if the gross mind still has desire, though one has withdrawn from worldly action, then one's actions are performed in the dreaming state when the body is as if paralyzed. Know, O Ram, when the mind performs action, but is yet free from it, that state is called the blissful Samadhi; the unchanging Nirvana and transcendent bliss.

"The two kinds of vision, meditation and non-meditation, are the results of the steady mind and the oscillating mind. Therefore, all the attributes of the mind must be controlled. It is said that meditation is the firm mind itself, devoid of desire or vexatious thoughts. Pain, internal or external, wears away in this Nirvanic state. A mind which is above its worries will reach Nirvana. Desires breed endless pain and misery in mental worry, and should therefore be relinquished.

"When all conception of 'I' among the multitude of visibles is vanquished, it does not matter where you live, O Ram, whether in a house, on a hillside or in the great forest. The blessed of quiescent mind, who have let go of egoism, find in the busiest household the solitude of the forest. They, who stroll in a street desiring nothing therein, really possess the street. Similarly, to those in full spiritual beatitude the city and the wood are the same. The forest retreat and the city abode become alike to him of introspective mind, and the functions of sleeping, waking or walking do not disturb this tranquillity of mind.

"O quiescent mind, twin of Prana, your cooling dew will chill the hot flowers of desire, and over all the universe shall be sweet peace. But should the mind become heated with the illusion of the world, then the hot breath of desire will sweep over the universe, like a great raging forest fire, leaving but ashes in its wake.

"The inner processes of mind are revealed in external actions. The earth, sky and air are all manifestations of the lower mind. He who loses himself in earthly joys will never enjoy the surpassing delight of Samadhi. But he who recognizes that the function of the lower mind must operate, but yet is aloof from mundane enjoyment, finds pure delight in Atma. He who lives in the life of others, spurning wealth, and seeing the world as it really is, is the real Knower.

"Whether death comes now or at the end of a cycle, these wise ones will never be corrupted in mind. The Vedas proclaim them as the blessed conquerors of the illusory conceptions of duality and belief in endings and beginnings, true enjoyers of bliss. By these characteristics, may we recognize those who have attained wisdom. But the recognition will not aid, O Ram, in the conception of the universal soul, for in words alone wisdom does not lie. Only in the divine word OM is Brahma hidden.

"O, benignant Ram, I shall relate to you a story which illustrates the attainment of Atmic wisdom. Hear you this history of Suragho, which is indeed wonderful.

"Suragho was a mighty hunter and ruler of the Kiratas. He lived with his people, who were adepts in archery, in the Kailasa Mountain on the summit of the Himalayas.

"Whilst he administered royal justice with strict impartiality, rewarding the righteous and punishing the wrongdoers, he soliloquized: 'If in the exercise of my royal power I afflict my people, are not their pains mine? Yet, if I do not punish them according to prescribed law, they shall have lived in vain. It is indeed a difficult task to rule over a kingdom.'

"The tender king was sorely troubled in mind.

"Muni Mandavya made a timely appearance. To him Suragho paid honor, and addressed the sage: 'O virtuous Muni, your coming fills me with happiness. It is indeed a blessing to know that I am in your notice. You have long been free from the melancholy of spirit. Help me to clear my mind of the misgivings that assail me. What else torments the mind of man more than doubt? My head is a whirl, O Muni, with the miseries and joys my subjects experience in obeying my will. Let the sun of wisdom light the darkness of my mind, and equality of vision comfort me.'

"Muni Mandavya replied: 'Atmic enquiry will clear away the fog of illusion, Suragho. Ask yourself ceaselessly, Who am I? Whence came the universe? Whence came birth and death? If you do this faithfully the reward of the Brahmic Seat shall be yours. When you make Atmic enquiry habitual, your mind will obey your will and you will cease your agonizing. To a poised mind the ups and downs of life appear trivial.

'Does the elephant flee at the sight of oxen tracks? What is of no consequence to the wise is appalling to others. For does not the rain, gathered in the footprint of a cow, seem an ocean of incalculable area to a mosquito? Know this, Suragho, that the farther removed you are from worldly distractions, the brighter the light of God illumines you. Just so long as you are engrossed in the affairs of the world, the true principle of God will not be recognized by you. Deific light will not shine when dualities still exist in the mind. It is as difficult to realize Atmic Reality, as to know that the alchemy of gold is not more to nature, than that of the baser metals. Therefore, longing for the things of the world must cease. The reward is the attainment of liberation—the supreme Brahmic state. O illustrious hunter, control your mind, and keep it free from bodily and unwise desires; so shall you then attain the stainless and beneficent Principle.'

"So saying Muni Mandavya returned to his own abode.

"The mighty hunter withdrew into his cave and in solitude began an inquiry into the origin of the ego. He thought, 'How absurd is it to call my body "I", for my body is composed of flesh and bone, which in its separate parts is passive. Hence my body is not "I". The ten organs of sense are other than the "I". I am not, then, the organs of my body. What remains is ego. What actuates my ego? Consciousness. But the universal consciousness cannot be termed the Reality. Therefore, I shall free myself from the Jiva state and become "THAT" which above all else, I desire to know. The fullness of wisdom, changeless and stainless, alone is my Reality. This transcendent Wisdom pervades all like the strand upon which pearls are strung,—Vishnu, Brahma, Devendra, Yama and all other states. This supreme and powerful Wisdom or Realization is not tainted by worldliness, is of divine aspect, and finds completion in all objects; has neither existence nor non-existence; is subtle and permeates all, even the abode of Truth where lives Brahma. This consciousness is the residual of all other potencies. It is due to motion or fluctuation of this consciousness, and to nothing else, that the diversified objects of this world are due.'

"Having relinquished the objective world and freed himself from the shackles of desire and delusion—delusion which follows one even in his seventh rebirth—Suragho maintained equality of vision, as one stationary in the Sushupti state. Free at last, though living in Atmic reality, he reached the Brahmic state and attained the status of a Brahman, like unto Raja Rishi Viswamitra, of extraordinary meditation.

"Thus did Suragho reach the Sushupti or dreamless state, wherein action is stilled, like a picture of a candle alight. In that state he was, and the opposites of love and hate, blessing or curse, association or separation, intelligence or ignorance, assailed him not."

Vashisht continued: "O Ram, hear also what took place between Suragho who attained, and a Raja Rishi named Parnada. Suragho had a friend, Parigha by name, of the race of Paraseeka, who was also a king. When Parigha's kingdom suffered a ten year drought, and famine and his people perished in great numbers, his heart gave way. He left his native country and went into a forest to meditate, denying himself food and subsisting upon dry leaves. Because of this he was called Parnada. Through the renunciation he practiced and his holy meditations, he attained Atmic wisdom, for none could compete with the strenuosities of this kingly recluse. This Muni, who traveled the three worlds as though he walked through the room of a dwelling, appeared before King Suragho. Each responded to the other's affectionate greeting and found pleasure in reciting their respective experiences.

"In welcome Suragho said: 'My heart overflows with joy and exquisite bliss. I hail you, O, honorable One.'

"Parnada answered: 'The sight of you lifts me into that Jnana state into which Muni Mandavya initiated you. O, King, are you able to direct your worldly affairs with equality and clarity of vision? Has your body, changed by the passing years, remained free from diseases, either physical or mental? Can you preserve your equilibrium of mind amid the inordinate luxuries of wealth? Have you been able to merge into Samadhi without thought, by following the paths of extreme serenity and solitude and forms actions or not, he who has Realized will always be poised in the Samadhic state. O Brother in Attainment, they who have not equanimity of mind will never be able to go into Samadhi, even though they sit in the Padme posture and offer salutations to Brahma. It is the fullness of Atmic wisdom which constitutes the noble Samadhi. If the mind controlled by concentration knows Reality, such a wise one may be said to enjoy Samadhi. The intelligence of the wise, free from illusion, yet mindful of worldly action, will not forget for a moment the eternity of Atmic Reality. As air flows freely in any direction, the wise intelligence will always follow the path of unchanging Atmic wisdom. The wise, who are in rapport with the indivisible Intelligence, having abandoned the illusion of the opposites except as worldly recognition is necessary, can be said to have attained the Brahmic Seat. Therefore, those blessed in wisdom, who refrain from too much consideration for bodily action, and who have enlivened the intelligence by the acquisition of holy knowledge, may penetrate everywhere. you have recognized the Intelligence which is wondrous and changeless. You have attained the Brahmic state. Your mind has been purged from worldliness, and your heart is liberated from egoism. Having known the certainty of Atma, you are complete and full in your Self.'

"Suragho replied: 'Of what avail are circuitous expressions? To say it briefly, it is this, when all longing for the fruits of action cease, and the mind looks upon all equally, being directed within itself, then Brahmic bliss arises, the incomparable Wise-Vision is developed, and the resolute Atmic Reality alone illumines.'"

Nine

THE LONG-LIVED YOGIN AND THE SECRET OF HIS LONGEVITY

⁓⸎⁓

Rishi Vashisht: "As there is no time, no place, the non-dual Brahma alone is radiating as Absolute Consciousness, without beginning or end; none else exists. With this in mind, you should not identify yourself with objects. Reaching the Jivan-mukta state, you may attain the non-dual latent silence and enjoy the final blessedness. So long as the ideas of ignorance remain with us, so long the Brahmic state will not be reached. As long as there is enjoyment of the illusory sense, the false creation of mind will continue. In fact, neither illusion, nor mind, nor ego exist, but the Shining One, Brahma, alone, which is like a Great Ocean rising and falling. As long as this 'I' identifies itself with the body, so long the illusions of the mind exist. So long as one has a love for possession of objects, so long the illusion of the mind will exist. If through the pure and eternal, the desire for the three worlds be sacrificed in the fire of Wisdom, then the illusion of mind will drop away. Those who are constantly meditating upon the All Pervading Self, which is the One Wisdom above material sense. looking with equal eye upon those who want to feed them and those who want to kill them, they may be said to have realized their Alma. Those who have meditated continually upon the Pure Wisdom and have put an end to the desires are like the sun which dispels darkness. Those who have known the real meaning of AUM (OM) as it should be known, will find. that their minds have become peaceful. Those who have dried to realize, but have not succeeded in seeing the Brahmic Principle, which is pure Wisdom, will be ever like a whirlwind in their mental attitude, or like a dry leaf in a storm.

"Though this Wisdom is imperishable, all beings do not try to attain it and are ever downcast. The egoist and the ignorant are attacking from all sides, like arrows on a battlefield. These worthless ones will kill their time, but will not try to find the imperishable True Wisdom. To the ignorant, the significance of OM is like unto casting a treasure into the ocean. All dangers are caused by the ignorant. No danger comes from the wise. This Maya is that which appears as the only reality to the ignorant. This world is as a shallow pool to the wise, but as a great ocean of pain to the ignorant.

"Reality cannot be realized by the senses. Out of this Reality, which is the witness of all an Intelligence arose, and subject to change, produced three states, the Finer, the Middle, and the Grosser. By these three qualities, Sattva (goodness, calmness),

Rajas (passion, motion) and Tamas (darkness, inertia), all beings are bound to rebirth. By rising above these three qualities, the Brahmic state is attained. This triune may be divided into nine classes each. Under the class of goodness are: Rishi, Munis, Nagas, Sidhas, Vidyadharas, Devas, and others. Nagas and Vidyadhara come under the Tamasic aspect of the Sattva. Sidhas and Munis come under the Rajasic aspect. All the others come under the Sattva aspect of Truthfulness. The Vidya (knowledge) arose out of Avidya (ignorance). This Vidya is no other than the Avidya itself. Again it is stated that Rajas and Tamas each have their three divisions. The Tamasic intelligence has to live within the ignorant body."

Ram asked: "How came the Intelligence to be entangled in the ignorant body?"

Rishi Vashisht replied: "The Intelligence, when it is without meditation, will first be as in a wild savage state; then it reaches the middle state between truth and untruth, and finally Wisdom, which has been lying dormant within the finer body. It will be idle as an indolent person without pains, until awakened by the Absolute One."

Ram asked: "Why not consider the fixed state of objects in the universe as liberation, as long as the Intelligence is in harmony with Oneness?"

Rishi Vashisht answered: "The attainment of the Oneness belongs to all beings. When one knows what is real and what is not real, that is the Supreme Liberation. When all desires have been sacrificed on the fire of Wisdom, then one attains the state of Oneness and Freedom.

"As a tree is in the seed, so are the desires within the heart. This is the dreamless state from which arose all rebirths, the cause of all desires within the heart. After the different worldly thoughts are killed, then the mischief maker - the cause of pains, goes to the dreamless state; but arises again and again like a tree from the seed, or dust from the earth. The unkilled desires will be hiding within the heart. This dreamless state, which is the mother of all desires, cannot be called liberation. The only one which is not the seed of that dreamless state is liberation or freedom. We should not be friendly to our enemy, namely impure desires, which like fire or poison, will ruin our life. The person who has done away with impure desires will never be affected by pain. The powers of mind are desires; its seed is ignorance. The wise stated that not to realize the eternal wisdom is the Avidya. Do away with all ignorance and unreality and become nondual. Believe that this universe is Brahma and not Avidya. To understand and see this universe as Brahma, alone is the emancipation. May you be blessed with that certain understanding which is found within the pure minds of Rishis and other great ones."

Ram asked: "Will you please enlighten me concerning the painless state of the Great One?"

The Teacher replied: "All varieties of things, whether large or small, are only Brahma. Wisdom is Brahma. We are Brahma. Our friends, kinsmen and our enemies are Brahma. To the blind this universe seems dark, but it is shining to those who have eyes to see; it is blissful to the wise, but painful to the ignorant. He, who sees and realizes this universe as Brahma, is Brahma himself; he will never miss immortality.

"The spotless is the self alone, which shines everywhere. That silent wisdom is Brahma, which will become a direct perception when a person sees only one alone. The wisdom which exists then is called the all-pervading wisdom of Brahma, and that is what we are. Let us call that, Atma, which gives us the fruits of all thoughts, which is the Light of Lights and which is neither with nor without qualities. Let us offer our solution to that Pure Wisdom which is devoid of all thoughts, pleasures or pains. Those who have conviction of the nothingness of thoughts and who act according to truth only, will enjoy the highest of the Brahmic state, which is filled with truth, quietness and equality. Those brave persons whose minds are filled with pure wisdom, and are looking with equal eyes over all, are free from desires, and will never become slaves of anything."

Ram then said: "Please explain the two paths through which the Jivanmukta has freed himself from all pains and desires.

Rishi Vashisht replied: "There are two methods of Yoga to overcome dire pains. The two are True Wisdom and the Control of Prana, which are given out by Parameshwara. To the constitution of some, Yoga is the most desirable; to the constitution of others, knowledge is preferable. These two, as I have explained, are based upon True Wisdom.

"Now I shall explain the meaning of Yoga. I shall tell you a beautiful story. Once upon a time I was in the company of other Rishis and heard from them the story of the long-lived

Yogin. A little hut was built on the top of the Kalpa Tree (a wish-fulfilling tree).

"This was a lofty one, on the northeast, side of the top of a big mountain. In that hut lived Bhusunde, a Yogin. There was no one in Heaven nor on earth who could sit with this Yogin in his practice of Yoga. This Yogin was the longest lived Yogin in the world, and was without desire. He possessed the wealth of liberation, and could see clearly the three periods of time. When the story was finished by the Great One in the assembly of the great, I was very eager to go and see personally, the long-lived Yogin. So I did, and saw the tree, the mountain with its slopes and caves and flowers in full bloom. On the tree were sitting many colored birds, some chanting Samaveda, others Mantras. Many parrots, kokilas, peacocks, and others. were developing in knowledge. Then I came before the long-lived Yogin, who was amid the-others. He was in perfect silence, without any motion of Prana and was enjoying bliss within himself. He came to greet me, and was overcome with joy when he recognized me. He welcomed me with kind words, and beautiful bunches of flowers which he produced by the power of his thought. He asked me to be seated, and showed me much kindness and courtesy. He said to me: 'I am overjoyed by your visit. you have taken a long journey. By your holy presence I have known all. All the learned ones think of me; therefore, you have come here, too. I wish to sip the nectar of your words.'

"I said: 'It is true, as you have stated, O King of birds. I came here to see you, who have been here a very long time. To what race do you trace your family? How did you attain pure Wisdom? How long have you been in the present body? What have you learned about Nature's laws? By which Wisdom have you been here? Please answer.'

"The long-lived One replied: 'In the best company of Supreme Shiva, who is elephant faced, sheep faced, camel faced, bear faced. Many of them have different heads, hands, etc. These elementals (beings) will encircle around Shiva at Kailasa Mountain. The Saktis powers will dance before Him, having their abode everywhere. These powers have different names, which are according to their degrees and forms. Once upon a time, a crow by the name of Chanda went to a meeting ordered by Shiva, where all Saktis get together to celebrate the great festival in the sky, where they dance and laugh with intoxication. The Chanda sported himself with the female swan (another Sakti), and by the joining of the two, the female swan became pregnant. When the dance was over, the pregnant swan of the power told of the conception to their head one. Thereupon, the Saktis spoke: 'You are impregnated by destiny. You will not be able to hold our pace, hence you must live according to your free will.' Saying this, Devi (divine mother) went to the highest Samadhi.

"'My mother and father lived on Manasa Lake, and I, and my twenty brothers and sisters were born there, lived with our parents, and worshipped the Brahma power for a long time. Devi awoke from her Samadhi and blessed us with her love—with liberation. Great peace was established within our hearts thereafter. In order to live alone without mixed associates, we said farewell to our parents. We attained liberation through the grace of a Sakti. We asked for a place where divine bliss could be enjoyed. We were directed to this place, giving thanks for the liberation, or freedom. We came here to live free from pain. All the karma I had made up to that date was now bearing fruit.

"'What will not be blessed by the Brahmic bliss? All good things arise by the grace of the wise. I am a knower of Brahma and will free myself soon of all material existence by your visit. This birth of mine is full of wonderful experiences. You know, as you are Iswara (God), himself. '

"I asked him how his brothers and sisters parted from him.

"The long-lived one responded: 'Here we lived for many yugas. At last my brothers and sisters were weary of the body and gave it up for liberation. They were blessed with great power and longevity and disappeared at will.'

"I asked him: 'How did you save yourself at the time of Pralaya, when the twelve suns melted all the universe?'

"The long-lived Yogin answered: 'Do you think that the actions of nature will ever stop? At the time of pralaya, when the twelve suns melted the universe, I gave up this place of mine and by the Dharana I went up to the sky. When the mountains burst forth, red hot rocks were thrown high into the air. I changed to the Fire Dharana (one who practices Fire Dharana cannot be burned by the fire). When all the world was sunk under the water, I floated by the Air Dharana. When the time came for the destruction of the universe, I took the Brahmic state and remained there until the beginning of creation over again. After the new creation, I returned again to this place. As for living, by my power, I rose above the mountains and created this tree.'

"I interrupted him and asked: 'By Dharana you preserved long life, while other Yogis perished?'

"The long-lived one answered: 'No, they did not perish, but they got tired of the burden of the human body and gave it up at will.'

"I asked him: 'You are master of all divine wisdom, and you see three worlds by the marvelous power of Yoga. I desire to know what you have seen.'

"The long lived one explained: 'For eleven thousand years of Devas there was one nebulous mass, devoid of anything. For the next four yugas, over 11,000,000 years, there was a forest; for the next four yugas, over 11,000,000 years, this earth was a chain of mountains; for the next four yugas this earth was overspread. Then Brahma became crafty and created by his will. At that time, men and women did as they liked. O Vashisht, I was witness to all these; the origin of the sun, etc. I saw Vishnu, one of the Trinity, who preserves, saving the earth and gathering together the Vedas that were scattered in all directions. You should know there have been countless Avatars, and it is difficult to count their number. O Great One, you have reincarnated eight times; this is our eighth meeting.

"'First, you were born of Akasa, then of fire, and then of water. I have witnessed this and seen great ones like Buddha reincarnated, and many others. The eternal Vedas will arise again and again in every age, as suited to human beings. They will understand it more and more.

"'As they advance, pure wisdom will be embodied in every yuga in the shape of Ramayana, like this one recited by Rishi Valmik. Twelve Valmiks had been before this one. They wrought the same wisdom in the form of Ramayana. Notable Vyasa composed Mahabhart. The Ram has been on this earth eleven times. He will incarnate again in the wealthy house. The illusion of this world sometimes will manifest, and other times not. All this illusion will be hidden within the Atma, as the foam in the ocean sometimes arises and again disappears. So I have seen the universe come and go.'

"I interrupted him by asking: 'When acting in a worldly way, how did you save yourself from the hands of death?'

"The long-lived one answered: 'What good will they gain if they will not act as the great ones have advised? I will explain to you. Yama (death) will not come to those whose minds are above pain. Death will not come to those who have mastered the serpent of desire. Yama will not come to those whose minds have attained peace; death will not come to those who have overcome the serpent of greed; yama will not come to those who have control of anger and passion; death will not tome to those who have reached the highest divine state by daily meditation; death will not come to those who have attained the non-dual state. Mental diseases and pain will not reach those who are non-dual, but have equal vision upon all.

"The mind should be kept under control. It should not become abstract on the way to reaching the highest state which is the Atma, or God, where no differentiation of this or that exists, having overcome all fear. Reaching this state is a difficult work, as it is all Bliss, without pain, and cannot be attained by the ignorant, who are roaming in the darkness. Wisdom is the way which leads to the state of highest bliss, the control of Prana, which is the way to control old age and death.'

"I then asked him: 'Will you please explain what it means to control Prana.'

"The long-lived one answered: 'Within this body, composed of the five elements, there are two vital forces, Prana and Apana. These two forces run smoothly, one upward and the other downward. Both are very fine forces and produce vibration. When these forces are arrested, then the Yogin can do the most wonderful things and know everything. One should always practice to control the Prana and Apana, as that leads to liberation and sets one free from rebirth.'

"'How can pain arise when one has mixed Apana in the Prana or Prana in the Apana? When Prana and Apana become as one, there will be no more pain or death. I followed this course. After controlling Prana, I attained the Supreme State. I do not care for the past nor the future, but only the present. I do not recognize that, by one course or another, I have succeeded in living a long life. I am all things to all men,—with the married I am married, with the suffering I suffer, with the happy I rejoice, as I am one with the whole universe.

"'My own life has been a happy one, free from pain, riches or poverty which do not affect me. My long life is due to the absence of egoism, and to your grace. With pure Wisdom I am blessed.'

"Thus did the long-lived one end his story. I said to him: 'I am enchanted with all that you have related. It is indeed marvelous. May your glory shine as the sun. May I start on my way.'

"So I started by air. He accompanied me many miles; then I forced him back to his palace. It was heart-rending to part with such a wise one.

"O Ram, this is the path of the Long-Lived Yogin."

Ten

THE GOAL OF THE YOGI AND LEVITATION

"Why is it that many Jivanmuktas do not have higher psychic powers developed, such as levitating in the air?" asked Ram.

Rishi Vashisht replied: "Those whose wisdom is not pure, but desire psychic powers are slaves of the world. The higher psychic powers are developed through Mantras, Postures, Mudras, but the true Jnani (truth seeker) does not seek or need the higher psychic powers. The truth seeker will ever try to attain the true vision of the Atma. The Jnani always tries to rest in wisdom but never goes in quest of psychic powers. Desire for worldly things or possessions are mere Maya.

"These Jnanis who have risen above Maya will never sink into it again. Jnanis who desire psychic power may develop it by Mantras, Postures, Mudras, etc., but psychic powers in their development will never bring beneficent liberation. That is the goal of the true Jnani. Desire for psychic powers tends to bondage; for that reason it will never appeal to the truth seeker.

"To those who have given up all desires, the Atma Jnana will arise without any doubt. But those who are after Sidhas only, which is the seed of desire, will never attain Atma."

"Please explain the secret of the Yogis who live as long as a Kalpa," asked Ram.

Rishi Vashisht answered: "As long as Prana is moving, the Yogin is moving, but When movement or Prana ceases, the Yogin becomes as immovable as a rock. Those Yogis who can control Prana may live as long as they desire. By controlling Prana, the mind also is controlled, externally and internally. He who controls Prana and mind arrests old age and death. Old age and death will never come near him. As the body becomes spiritualized, it will never retrograde.

"Those Yogis only can be said to have found the Reality, who always follow the path of Atma Jnani. They, who have given up all their desires and have been liberated from mental bonds, are free."

"By giving up all desires, the mind is merged into its Reality; then what becomes of the gunas?" asked Ram, of the Teacher.

Rishi Vashisht answered: "There are two ways in which the mind may be controlled, as the mind consists of the formless and the formed. By controlling the Rupa (with form) mind, one will bring about the Jivanmukti state. By controlling Arupa (formless) mind, one will bring the Videhmukti state (emancipation of the Soul).

"Uncontrolled Rupa mind generates all kinds of pain. But by control bliss will come. You must master this Rupa mind, as it identifies itself with matter. Then it is not able to find its Reality, and therefore it brings pain. This form mind is the ego. This form mind is ever involved in pleasures and pain. It is the seed of Maya. This will give you the idea of the Rupa mind.

"Now I will deal with the controlling of the mind. Please listen. It is said by the wise that the fruitless mind can be controlled by looking with equal eyes upon all, and not being affected by pleasure or pain. As the mountain is not affected by the storm, also one is able to retain his poise in the presence of riches or poverty, joy or sorrow. Of such a person it may be said; he has control over his mind; he has overcome ignorance, which is the lower mind itself. Through control it brings out high spiritual intelligence. Such a mind does not subject itself to rebirth. By the desires of the gunas, one will come to the state which belongs to the Jivanmukta or liberation in this life.

"This Rupa mind is the destroyer of the peace. In this mind the gunas will grow as the lotus in the lake. By controlling the Arupa, one may gain the state of Videhmukti. This state will be attained by overcoming the gunas known as: Sattva, Raja, Tamas.

"There is no other way of controlling the Arupa mind, than doing away with differences. The Brahmic state is that in which one does not see differences. What has or has not been, that which has or has not qualities, which has or has not wealth, contentment or discontentment, light or darkness, day or night.

"This state is the home of those who have conquered all desires toward this universe. One becomes like Akasa or air, which is not affected, but takes on odors. These great Yogis, living as if their bodies were Akasa are in the Brahmic state, that is all bliss. Pain, pleasure, name or fame does not affect them in any way. These great ones have controlled their minds."

"What is its seed? What is the seed of this seed? And what is the seed of the last one?" asked Ram.

Rishi Vashisht answered: "The body is the first seed, it generates all pleasure and pain. It gives rise to the ever revolving Samsara (material world governed by the cycle of death and rebirth). The seed of this seed is the mind, which always pursues the track of desires and is the cause of pleasure and of pain, birth and death. By the mind, hosts of bodies are generated, which seem to exist though they do not exist. It enjoys these bodily objects as if in a dream.

"To this mind, which is always surrounded or encircled by the worldly action, there are two seeds. One is desire, the other is Prana. These are the four seeds. O Ram, the all-pervading one wisdom becomes the visible wisdom, by the motion of Prana. If this Prana stopped expanding in every direction, then it would attend to one's welfare and progress.

"The intelligence becomes attached to the visible world by

desire. The visible world is the root of all misery. If the intelligence could always remain in the dreamless state, without lapsing into the dreaming state, that would be the real Nirvana or the Atma. It would result in liberation, or freedom from rebirth.

"If the desire for sensual objects, which arise through the Prana movement are gradually controlled, the accumulation of these thoughts will constitute the mind. With such a mind alone, people live in this world. For controlling this kind of mind, the wise and the Yogin practice or perform Pranayama. Pranayama is the practice of controlling Prana and concentration. The wise say that the benefit of control of the Prana brings the equality of mind—the ability to look upon all as one. This generates blessed joy and not pain.

"The seed of the mind seed is the ego, which with its partner, desire, enjoys the external objects. The desires make people slaves of the sensual objects. The power of true discrimination is developed through firm determination. If this power is lost, the ego or false self binds itself to the mercy of desires, which make it see real as unreal and unreal as real. The power of desire makes everything appear in an illusory light. This mind is most disgraceful, as it identifies the 'I' with that which is not 'I'. Through this mind, old age, death and birth are brought about.

"As the oscillating of the mind arises through its confusion with objects, birth and death also arise. It is only when this mind is subdued and has no more attraction or repulsion toward objects, that it will cease oscillating.

"If thoughts are controlled by giving up desires, the result will surely be peace of mind. If there is no desire for worldly things, then how can this mind go roaming in the sky? O Ram!

"I think so long as sensual thought exists in the mind, so long will desires remain. The idea of their reality, and the enjoyment of pleasure therein, can be said to be the thought of the mind. All thought or desire makes karma.

"How can the mind oscillate in the wise, who are purer than ether, and have risen above desires? It is said, that the realization of Reality by one who understands true discrimination, is that he is not in this material world, and the world is all Maya, made by the mind.

"The wise say that the mind denudes itself of its form, even though it is engaged in actions. When the mind has dissolved all things into itself, then it becomes as cool and refreshing as ambrosia. Those Jivanmuktas who have freed themselves from desires, will live to wear out their past karma. Those Jivanmuktas are in possession of pure desires, without any pain or rebirth. It is these emancipated ones, whose minds have found the Reality of Being, and have reached the highest wisdom. It is these Jivanmuktas who, when they give up the body, attain the highest state, as they are the lofty ones.

"The two seeds of mind as has been stated before, are the desires, and the movement of Prana, and if one of them is controlled, both are controlled. By desire, Prana is moved, and by Prana desire is moved. Therefore, we may say that these seed motions of Prana and desire are the dried fruits of the mind, and their roots are in the external world. Hence, if they are released from the external world, then the movement of Prana and desires are also controlled. The mental actions are the seeds of the eternal world. If intelligence does not play its part in the external world, then the external world will cease to exist. As the sesame oil cannot exist without the sesame seed, so the existence of the external and the internal are not different.

"The awakening of pure wisdom will produce a kind of creation, through which pure wisdom will see in itself the external objects. As in a dream, though one forgets himself, still he sees things in himself by some inherent power, so the external is known by mental knowledge. Those who by their knowledge of discrimination control this reflected mind, whether they have analyzed it or not, will also control disease and death. It is the non-control of the reflection of the external, that puts us into the great universe, but through its control the goal is attained. Who can say that the external does not bring great pain upon us, O Ram?

"Through the absence of the external and the non-relation of objects, divine bliss arises. You may stop your mind from oscillating, give up all love for worldly enjoyment, forget the objective world, and still not be in a dull state. You are above the Paramatma. In the wisdom state, the external is not seen. This is true without doubt."

Ram asked: "How can non-intelligence arise, where there is no visible or external? How can the external or visible vanish, from where there is no wisdom?"

Rishi Vashisht answered: "Atma is the All-pervading One, without any attraction. It has no power of knowing nor not-knowing. Any inert object is without the visible or objective. If Atma attains, then that wisdom will not be mixed with the visible or objective. It will stand alone. Though engaged in all actions, it will not be affected by the visible or objective. He alone is the Jnani; he alone is the Jivanmukta. At this stage when all external subjects are given up, he attains full Atmic Wisdom, without any mental knowledge. Then he will not be attached to any object, but liberated front pain through Divine Bliss, or Samadhi. He will have all bliss. A truth seeker should always cling to such meditation, without longing for the unreal, and he will always enjoy himself in his own Blessed Atma, whether walking, talking or working. He will be above all of those conditions, as they have no attraction for him. He is not attracted by the external with its enjoyment, but lives in consciousness of perfect bliss.

"Understand thoroughly this wisdom, and you become conscious of the truth that you are the All-pervading Wisdom itself, after rising above the sea of pain, although engaged in worldly activities.

"To this wisdom the Eternal Absolute is the seed. Out of this Oneness, wisdom arises as the light from a flame. The Oneness has two appearances. Now, I shall explain them; jars, vases and other objects appear to be different, but still they are all one, as they are all made of earth. The seat of the Truth is in Oneness alone, non-dual, without any attributes. Therefore, you should be free from the three elements—time, space, and causation, and sink yourself into the Eternal Absolute. Time, space and causation seem to be three different elements in their action, but they belong to Oneness. These three elements are the cause of creating diversified action in this world.

"Meditate alone upon the Non-dual or Oneness which is common to all. You may pervade everywhere with the Self-bliss, that which is the goal of Oneness. That state is the seed of this pure Oneness. From this Oneness the universal consciousness arises. From this point all thought of doubt vanishes, and one gains a blessed consciousness, of ever present joy. This is the primal seed, but there is no seed to the state of Pure Wisdom. He, who is capable of holding the Pure Wisdom without wavering, will never sink himself into illusion. This is the cause of all, but it is a causeless cause. It is the essence of all, but there is no essence to it.

"In this great glass (the Self), all things will appear as images, as do the trees in the bank of a lake, where they are reflected in the water. This is the Pure One. It alone is the ageless; it alone is the Atmic Reality. By attaining this state, the mind will become peaceful. May you, after realizing it firmly, become that Atma. May you attain that Nirvanic state."

Ram said to the Teacher: "You have been kind enough to explain about the nature of four seeds. With what effort, can one attain that state of bliss and wisdom?"

Rishi Vashisht replied: "By proper efforts in the direction of overcoming those seeds, and the cause of the pains, which I have explained, the state of bliss and wisdom may be attained. To reach that state is the highest of all other states, and is the common goal of all. You will have to give up the entire host of desires, for if any are left lingering with you, it may be a hindrance to your progress. Realize your Higher Self, and at that very moment, you will have attained that highest state. Should that Oneness, just referred to, be first attained by you, then, with a little more effort you will attain the highest state. Therefore, direct your meditation toward attainment of this state of Oneness, and the rest will follow.

"O Ram, it is difficult indeed, to reach this blissful state, as long as one clings to the external world. With all your might you should endeavor to give up the idea of duality and desires, then, all mental discord, disease and pain will vanish. One will find it as difficult to control the desires, as to remove the mountain. As long as the desires are not controlled, the mind will be uncontrolled. As long as the mind is not mastered, so long desires will not be mastered, as they are one. As long as Pure Wisdom has not arisen, so long the desires will be uncontrolled. Pure Wisdom, the controlling power of mind and mastery of desires, is naturally dependent upon no other cause than itself, for its control or mastery. It is by effort of his will, that the Yogin walks in the right path."

GLOSSARY

Samsara - An ordinary world of suffering and cyclical birth and death

Ajnani - Unlearned, ignorant

Akasa - Ether element, space

Arupa - Formless, non-physical object. See Rupa

Atma - Individual soul, self

Atmic Reality - Highestl level of reality and consciousnes

Atmic Tattva - Highest wisdom of the self

Avidya - Ignorance. See Vidya

AUM - See OM

Brahma - Ultimate reality, the truth. The God of creation. One of the main deities from the Hindu Trinity

Bhairava - A Hindu deity associated with annihilation. A ferocious manifestation of Shiva

Bharatavarsa - Land of India

Buddhi - The intellectual faculty, reasoning

Chidakasa - Space of consciousness. See Akasha

Chintamuni - A wish-fulfilling jewel

Devi - Goddess, Divine Mother

Dharana - The practice of concentration of the mind

Gunas - Three qualities of matter. See Sattva, Rajas and Tamas

Guru - A spiritual teacher

Japa Chanting - Chanting of sacred mantras

Jivanmukta - State of emancipated embodiment, full liberation. Emancipated beings.

Jnan - Wisdom, spiritual knowledge

Jnanendriya - Organs of sense

Jnani - Truth seeker

Iswara - Lord, God

Kailasa mountain - The holiest mountain in the Himalayas. Abode of Shiva

Kalpa Tree - A wish-fulfilling divine tree

Kalpa - A long period of time (aeon) in Hindu and Buddhist cosmology, generally between the creation and recreation of a world or universe

Karma - Destiny or fate, following as effect from cause. Actions

Karmaendriya - Organs of action

Kiratas - Generic term that refers to people who had territory in the mountains, particularly in the Himalayas

Lakshmi - A Hindu Goddess of prosperity, fortune and wealth

Mahameru Mountain - Sacred five-peaked mountain of Hindu cosmology. The center of all the physical, metaphysical and spiritual universes

Maya - Illusory sense-world of manifold phenomena to conceal the unity of absolute being

Muni - A holy man, sage, ascetic

Nirvana - Liberation from the sense-world, cessation of

suffering

OM - Sacred mantra. The primordial sound that refers to Atma and Brahma

Parabrahma - Supreme Spirit. Highest Self

Paramatma - Absolute, Supreme Self, Universal Soul

Parameshwara - Supreme God

Pralaya - A period of dissolution or destruction of the manifested universe at the end of a kalpa

Prana - Vital force

Rajas - One of three gunas. Stands for passion, motion

Rishi - A Hindu sage or saint

Rudra - Another name for Shiva

Rupa - A material form, physical object. See Arupa

Sakti - A divine energy, power

Samadhi - Highest meditation state at which Oneness is attaned

Samayan - Highest power of the Raja Yogin

Saptarishi - Well known seven Rishis who appear throughout Vedas texts

Saraswati - A Hindu Goddess of knowledge, music, art, speech, and wisdom

Sastaric - The right path

Sattva - One of the three gunas. Stands for goodness, calmness

Shiva - The God of destruction and regeneration. One of the main deities from the Hindu Trinity

Sidhas - Great Yogins, masters of psychic power who attained Oneness

Sushupti - Dreamless state

Tamas - One of the three gunas. Stands for darkness, inertia

Tapas - Religious austerities

Tat Twamasi - Sanskrit for *You are that*

Turya - State of wakeful sleep

Veda - Sacred Knowledge

Vedas - Four books of Wisdom

Videhmukti - State of the emancipation of the Soul

Vidya - Knowledge. See Avidya

Vishnu - The God of preservation. One of the main deities from the Hindu Trinity

Yama - The God of death

Yuga - A cyclic age, epoch, in Hindu cosmology. Each cycle lasts for 4,320,000 years